Delinquent Boys

THE CULTURE OF THE GANG

by Albert K. Cohen

THE FREE PRESS
A Division of Macmillan Publishing Co., Inc.
New York

Collier Macmillan Publishers
London

Dedicated

To My Parents

The Free Press
A DIVISION OF MACMILLAN PUBLISHING CO., INC.
866 Third Avenue, New York, N.Y. 10022

Collier Macmillan Canada, Ltd.

Library of Congress Catalog Card Number: 55-7337

First Free Press Paperback Edition 1971

Printed in the United States of America

printing number
8   9   10

Contents

Preface

TO ENUMERATE all those on whose work I have built or who, through criticism and suggestion, have influenced the conception or the writing of this book would be impossible. I must, however, acknowledge my special indebtedness to the late Edwin H. Sutherland of Indiana University and to Talcott Parsons and Robert F. Bales of Harvard University. For her generous assistance in the typing of the manuscript, I wish to express my gratitude to Mrs. Jean Beckhorn.

CHAPTER I

An Unsolved Problem
in Juvenile Delinquency

THE EXPRESSION, "the delinquent subculture," may be new to some readers of this volume. The idea for which it stands, however, is a commonplace of folk—as well as scientific—thinking. When Mrs. Jones says: "My Johnny is really a good boy but got to running around with the wrong bunch and got into trouble," she is making a set of assumptions which, when spelled out more explicitly, constitute the foundations of an important school of thought in the scientific study of juvenile delinquency. She is affirming that delinquency is neither an inborn disposition nor something the child has contrived by himself; that children *learn* to become delinquents by becoming members of groups in which delinquent conduct is already established and "the thing to do"; and that a child need not be "different" from other children, that he need not have any twists or defects of personality or intelligence in order to become a delinquent.

In the language of contemporary sociology, she is saying that juvenile delinquency is a subculture. The concept "culture" is familiar enough to the modern layman. It refers to knowledge, beliefs, values, codes, tastes and prejudices that are traditional in social groups and that are acquired by participation in such groups. Our American language, political habits, sex mores, taste for hamburger and cokes and aversion to horse meat are parts of American culture. We take for granted that the contrasting ways of Hindus, Chinese and Navahos are for the most part a matter of indoctrination into a different culture. But the notion of culture is not limited to the distinctive ways of life of such large-scale national and tribal societies. Every society is internally differentiated into numerous sub-groups, each with ways of thinking and doing that are in some respects peculiarly its own, that one can acquire only by participating in these sub-groups and that one can scarcely help acquiring if he is a full-fledged participant. These cultures within cultures are "subcultures." Thus, within American society we find regional differences in speech, cookery, folklore, games, politics and dress. Within each age group there flourish subcultures not shared by its juniors or elders. The rules of marbles and jackstones live on, long after you and I have forgotten them, in the minds of new generations of children. Then there are subcultures within subcultures. There is the subculture of a factory and of a shop with the factory; the subculture of a university and of a fraternity within the university; the subculture of a neighborhood and of a family, clique or gang within the neighborhood. All these subcultures have this in common: they are acquired only by interaction with those who already share and embody, in their belief and action, the culture pattern.

When we speak of a delinquent subculture, we speak of a way of life that has somehow become traditional among certain groups in American society. These groups are the boys' gangs that flourish most conspicuously in the "delinquency neighborhoods" of our larger American cities. The members of these gangs grow up, some to become law-abiding citizens and others to graduate to more professional and adult forms of criminality, but the delinquent tradition is kept alive by the age-groups that succeed them. This book is an attempt to answer some important questions about this delinquent subculture. The pages which follow will prepare the ground for the formulation of these questions.

A large and growing number of students of juvenile delinquency, systematically developing the implications of Mrs. Jones' explanation of Johnny's "trouble," believes that the only important difference between the delinquent and the non-delinquent is the degree of exposure to this delinquent culture pattern. They hold that the delinquent is not distinguished by any special stigmata, physical or psychological. Some delinquents are bright, some are slow; some are seriously frustrated, some are not; some have grave mental conflicts and some do not. And the same is true of non-delinquents. Delinquency, according to this view, is not an expression or contrivance of a particular kind of personality; it may be imposed upon any kind of personality if circumstances favor intimate association with delinquent models. The process of becoming a delinquent is the same as the process of becoming, let us say, a Boy Scout. The difference lies only in the cultural pattern with which the child associates.[1]

In describing this "cultural-transmission" theory of juvenile delinquency we have already suggested the main features of its principal rival. Mrs. Jones' neighbor may be of a different mind about Johnny's delinquency. "That kid's just never been trained to act like a human being! If I let my kid run wild like Johnny, if I never laid down the law to him, he'd be the same way. Any kid will steal and raise cane if you don't teach him right from wrong and if you let him get away with anything." Or her explanation may run like this: "He never had a chance. The way he's been tossed from pillar to post! The way his folks have always fought with one another and the way they've both beat on him! The one thing he's never had is a little real love. What do you expect of a boy when his own people treat him like dirt and the whole family is all mixed up?"

Again, if we spell out the assumptions underlying these two "explanations," we find that they are two variants of a whole class of theories which we may call "psychogenic." These are the theories which are favored by psychiatrists, especially those of a psychoanalytic persuasion. These theories have in common the idea that delinquency is a result of some attribute of the personality of the child, an attribute which the non-delinquent child does not possess or does not possess in the same degree. One type of psychogenic theory holds that every human being is endowed with a fund of inborn or instinctual anti-social impulses, commonly called the Id. Most people, in the course of growing up, acquire a capacity for circumspection or prudence, commonly called the Ego. They also incorporate into their own personalities, as conscience or Superego, the moral code of their society. The Ego and Superego together normally suffice to hold the Id in check. The delinquent and the criminal differ from the normal, law-abiding person in the possession of unusually imperious Id drives or faulty Ego or Superego development, resulting in the eruption of the Id into illegal acts. This imperfect mastery of the Id may be a result of faulty training or parental neglect. Here we recognize the substance of our neighbor lady's first explanation: Johnny's Ego and Superego, through the failure of his family to train and discipline him, are too weak to restrain his bumptious Id.[2]

Another type of psychogenic theory does not assume that the impulse to delinquency is itself inborn. Rather, it views delinquency as a symptom of, or a method of coping with, some underlying problem of adjustment. The delinquent differs from the non-delinquent in that he has frustrations, deprivations, insecurities, anxieties, guilt feelings or mental conflicts which differ in kind or degree from those of non-delinquent children. The delinquency is often thought of as related to the underlying problem of adjustment as a fever is related to the underlying infection. Our neighbor lady's second explanation is a folksy version of this mental conflict variant of psychogenic theory: as a result of a disturbed family situation, Johnny is "mixed up," he has psychological problems, and these problems find their expression through delinquency.[3]

Psychogenic theories of both classes recognize the importance of the child's social environment in producing the character structure or the problem of adjustment, but give it relatively little weight in determining the particular manner in which it finds expression. For the first class of psychogenic theories, the Id is already there at birth in all people. It does not *become* criminal through experience. It is criminal from the very start and never changes. What is acquired through experience is the shell of inhibition. For the second class, delinquency as a symptom or mode of adjustment is contrived or "hit upon" by the child himself, perhaps through one or more of the familiar "mechanisms" of substitution, regression, displacement, compensation, rationalization and projection. If other children exhibit the same behavior it is because they have *independently contrived* the same solution.

We have been discussing kinds of theories. It does not follow that all students of juvenile delinquency embrace one or another of them as an explanation for all delinquency. On the contrary, most students give at least passing acknowledgment to more than one kind of causal process. Thus, many psychoanalysts, the people most strongly wedded to psychogenic theories, recognize the existence of a kind of delinquent who is not just giving expression to his Id or working out a problem of adjustment but who has internalized a "delinquent Superego." That is, he has internalized the moral code of his group and is acting in accordance with that code, but it happens

internalized delinq. code

to be a delinquent code. It is fairly typical of psychoanalytical writers, however, that they formally concede, so to
speak, the existence of this sort of thing but thereafter, in
their actual case studies, pay little attention to it.[4] At the
same time most sociologists, who are generally disposed
to favor a cultural-transmission theory, feel that there are
some delinquents whose delinquency cannot be explained
in cultural-transmission terms. Many of these sociologists,
however, are reluctant to flirt with psychogenic alternatives, particularly those of the more extreme psychoanalytical kind.

It may be that we are confronted with a false dicho-
tomy, that we are not really forced to choose between two
conflicting theories. There is the possibility of two or more
"types" of juvenile delinquents, each the result of a different kind of etiology or causal process: one, let us say,
predominantly subcultural and another predominantly
psychogenic.[5] There is the possibility of subcultural and
psychogenic "factors" simultaneously but independently
at work in the same personality, each providing a separate
and distinct "push" in the direction of delinquency, like
two shoulders to the same wheel. However, we are especially interested in a third possibility, namely, that in the
majority of cases psychogenic and subcultural factors
blend in a single causal process, as pollen and a particular
bodily constitution work together to produce hay fever.
If this is so, then the task of theory is to determine the
ways in which the two kinds of factors mesh or interact.
We will have a good deal to say about this as our inquiry
unfolds.

In the present state of our knowledge, there is room for question and disagreement about the proportion of all juvenile delinquency which depends, in some way, upon participation in the delinquent subculture; about the relationship between cultural-transmission and psychogenic factors; and about the nature of the culture-transmission process itself, that is, about just how persons take over a new subculture. There seems to be no question, however, but that there is a delinquent subculture, and that it is a normal, integral and deeply-rooted feature of the social life of the modern American city.

Now we come to a curious gap in delinquency theory. Note the part that the existence of the delinquent subculture plays in the cultural-transmission theories. It is treated as a *datum*, that is, as something which already exists in the environment of the child. The problem with which these theories are concerned is to *explain how that subculture is taken over by the child.* Now we may ask: Why is there such a subculture? Why is it "there" to be "taken over"? Why does it have the particular content that it does and why is it distributed as it is within our social system? Why does it arise and persist, as it does, in such dependable fashion in certain neighborhoods of our American cities? Why does it not "diffuse" to other areas and to other classes of our population? Similar questions can be asked about any subculture: the values and argot of the professional dance band musician, social class differences in religious beliefs and practice, the distinctive subcultures of college campuses. Any subculture calls for explanation in its own right. It is never a random growth. It has its characteristic niche in our social structure; elsewhere it does not "catch on." It has its characteristic flavor, qualities, style. Why these and not others?

With respect to the delinquent subculture, these questions are of more than theoretical or speculative interest alone. Social control of juvenile delinquency is a major practical problem of every sizable American community. No such efforts at control have thus far proved spectacularly successful. While knowledge does not guarantee power, it is improbable that we will achieve striking successes at control without some understanding of the sources and sustenance of this subculture in our midst. The problem has not, to be sure, been completely ignored but there has been remarkably little effort to account for the delinquent subculture itself. That is the task of this book. A by-product of our inquiries will be a new perspective on the issue of psychogenic *versus* cultural-transmission theories of delinquency.

CHAPTER II

Facts the Theory Must Fit

INTRODUCTION

IN THE social sciences many ingenious efforts at explanation have come to grief because they failed to respect a platitudinous but important truth: if one wants to explain some thing which has a number of distinct parts, his explanation must fit all the parts and not just some facet of the thing which happens, for some reason, to intrigue him. Indeed, if he fails to keep in mind the whole, he is not likely to find a satisfactory explanation of the part. This is because any detail, taken by itself, can often admit of a number of different and equally plausible explanations. To adjudicate among these alternatives we must determine which of them is most consistent with *the rest of the facts* which make up the remainder of the concrete totality. But we are all too prone to become beguiled by some particular characteristic, perhaps because it is the most spectacular or the most annoying or because it lends itself most easily to plausible speculation. Preoccupied thus with details and ignoring contexts, we proceed to expend our energies and ingenuity on constructing shaky or irrelevant theories.

For example "prostitution" is more than "sexual immorality," for "sexual immorality" takes many forms, including adultery, homosexuality and other "perversions," premarital sexual relations with one's fiancé, and heterosexual "promiscuity" with no view to financial gain. None of these things is "prostitution"; no explanation of any of these things explains "prostitution," although the explanation may contain elements that are part of the explanation of "prostitution." Again, divorce is not explained by explaining dissatisfaction in marriage, for dissatisfaction in marriage has other issues than divorce. And an explanation of embezzlement which focuses on the sheer criminality of the act but fails to explain why some people become embezzlers rather than some other kind of criminal is not a satisfactory explanation of embezzlement.

We see, then, why our first task must be to set forth clearly the different characteristics of the delinquent subculture, the thing we are trying to explain. In one way, this simplifies our task. Not all crime, not even all juvenile crime, will fit this description of the delinquent subculture. We will thus have limited our undertaking and cannot be held responsible for failing to explain that which clearly falls outside of the task area we have staked out. Parenthetically, we may also remark that it would be exceedingly presumptuous for us to attempt to resolve, in one small volume, all the problems in the vast area of juvenile delinquency. In another way, it makes our task more exacting. The thoughtful critic will bear in mind our description of the delinquent subculture. Should our theory seem to account plausibly for some of the characteristics of the delinquent subculture but not for others, he will confront us with our own description and require of us a defense or modification of our theory such that it accounts truly for the delinquent subculture in all its richness and detail.

In the following pages we present a portrait of the delinquent subculture. In presenting a thumbnail description of any widely distributed subculture it is impossible to do full justice to the facts, for no brief account can deal with all the varieties and nuances which actually exist. The subcultures of the medical profession, the professional gambler or the jitterbug have many local versions, as does the delinquent subculture. Nonetheless, it is possible, for each of these subcultures, to draw a picture which represents certain themes or traits which run through all the variants. This "ideal-typical" or 'full-blown" picture will be fully realized in some of the variants and only approximated, in various degrees, in others. This much, however, may be said for our description of the delinquent subculture. It is a real picture, drawn from life. It is the picture most familiar to students of juvenile delinquency, especially those who, like the group worker, encounter the delinquent gang in its natural habitat, the streets and alleys of our cities. It is the picture that stands out most prominently in the literature of juvenile delinquency. Compare it to a generalized picture of a pear, in which the distinctively pearlike features are accentuated. Many pears will look very like our picture; others will only approximate it. However, if our picture is truly drawn, it will give us a good idea of the shape which distinguishes pears in general from other fruits. This is the kind of validity which we claim for our portrait of the delinquent subculture.

THE CONTENT OF THE DELINQUENT SUBCULTURE

THE COMMON EXPRESSION, "juvenile crime," has unfortunate and misleading connotations. It suggests that we have two kinds of criminals, young and old, but only one kind of crime. It suggests that crime has its meanings and its motives which are much the same for young and old; that the young differ from the old as the apprentice and the master differ at the same trade; that we distinguish the young from the old only because the young are less "set in their ways," less "confirmed" in the same criminal habits, more amenable to treatment and more deserving, because of their tender age, of special consideration.

The problem of the relationship between juvenile delinquency and adult crime has many facets. To what extent are the offenses of children and adults distributed among the same legal categories, "burglary," "larceny," "vehicle-taking," and so forth? To what extent, even when the offenses are legally identical, do these acts have the same meaning for children and adults? To what extent are the careers of adult criminals continuations of careers of juvenile delinquency? We cannot solve these problems here, but we want to emphasize the danger of making facile and unproven assumptions. If we assume that "crime is crime," that child and adult criminals are practitioners of the same trade, and if our assumptions are false, then the road to error is wide and clear. Easily and unconsciously, we may impute a whole host of notions concerning the nature of crime and its causes, derived from our knowledge and fancies about adult crime, to a large realm of behavior to which these notions are irrelevant. It is better to make no such assumptions; it is better to look at juvenile delinquency with a fresh eye and try to explain what we see.

What we see when we look at the delinquent subculture (and we must not even assume that this describes *all juvenile* crime) is that it is *non-utilitarian, malicious* and *negativistic.*

We usually assume that when people steal things, they steal because they want them. They may want them because they can eat them, wear them or otherwise use them; or because they can sell them; or even—if we are given to a psychoanalytic turn of mind—because on some deep symbolic level they substitute or stand for something unconsciously desired but forbidden. All of these explanations have this in common, that they assume that the stealing is a means to an end, namely, the possession of some object of value, and that it is, in this sense, rational and "utilitarian." However, the fact cannot be blinked—and this fact is of crucial importance in defining our problem

—that much gang stealing has no such motivation at all. Even where the value of the object stolen is itself a motivating consideration, the stolen sweets are often sweeter than those acquired by more legitimate and prosaic means. In homelier language, stealing "for the hell of it" and apart from considerations of gain and profit is a valued activity to which attaches glory, prowess and profound satisfaction. There is no accounting in rational and utilitarian terms for the effort expended and the danger run in stealing things which are often discarded, destroyed or casually given away. A group of boys enters a store where each takes a hat, a ball or a light bulb. They then move on to another store where these things are covertly exchanged for like articles. Then they move on to other stores to continue the game indefinitely. They steal a basket of peaches, desultorily munch on a few of them and leave the rest to spoil. They steal clothes they cannot wear and toys they will not use. Unquestionably, most delinquents are from the more "needy" and "underprivileged" classes, and unquestionably many things are stolen because they are intrinsically valued. However, a humane and compassionate regard for their economic disabilities should not blind us to the fact that stealing is not merely an alternative means to the acquisition of objects otherwise difficult of attainment.[1]

Can we then account for this stealing by simply describing it as another form of recreation, play or sport? Surely it is that, but why is this form of play so attractive to some and so unappealing to others? Mountain climbing, chess, pinball, number pools and bingo are also different kinds of recreation. Each of us, child or adult, can choose from a host of alternative means for satisfying our common "need" for recreation. But every choice expresses a preference, and every preference reflects something about the chooser or his circumstances that endows the object of his choice with some special quality or virtue. The choice is not self-explanatory nor is it arbitrary or random. Each form of recreation is distributed in a characteristic way among the age, sex and social class sectors of our population. The explanation of these distributions and of the way they change is often puzzling, sometimes fascinating and rarely platitudinous.

By the same logic, it is an imperfect answer to our problem to say: "Stealing is but another way of satisfying the universal desire for status." Nothing is more obvious from numberless case histories of subcultural delinquents that they steal to achieve recognition and to avoid isolation or opprobrium. This is an important insight and part of the foundation on which we shall build. But the question still haunts us: "Why is stealing a claim to status in one group and a degrading blot in another?"

If stealing itself is not motivated by rational, utilitarian considerations, still less are the manifold other activities which constitute the delinquent's repertoire. Throughout there is a kind of *malice* apparent, an enjoyment in the discomfiture of others, a delight in the defiance of taboos itself. Thrasher quotes one gang delinquent:

We did all kinds of dirty tricks for fun. We'd see a sign, "Please keep the streets clean," but we'd tear it down and say, "We don't feel like keeping it clean." One day we put a can of glue in the engine of a man's car. We would always tear things down. That would make us laugh and feel good, to have so many jokes.*

The gang exhibits this gratuitous hostility toward non-gang peers as well as adults. Apart from its more dramatic manifestations in the form of gang wars, there is keen delight in terrorizing "good" children, in driving them from playgrounds and gyms for which the gang itself may have little use, and in general in making themselves obnoxious to the virtuous. The same spirit is evident in playing hookey and in misbehavior in school. The teacher and her rules are not merely something onerous to be evaded. They are to be *flouted*. There is an element of active spite and malice, contempt and ridicule, challenge and defiance, exquisitely symbolized, in an incident described to the writer by Mr. Henry D. McKay, of defecating on the teacher's desk.[2]

All this suggests also the intention of our term "negativistic." The delinquent subculture is not only a set of rules, a design for living which is different from or indifferent to or even in conflict with the norms of the "respectable" adult society. It would appear at least plausible that it is defined by its "negative polarity" to those norms. That is, the delinquent subculture takes its norms from the larger culture but turns them upside down. The delinquent's conduct is right, by the standards of his subculture, precisely *because* it is wrong by the norms of the larger culture.[3] "Malicious" and "negativistic" are foreign to the delinquent's vocabulary but he will often assure us,

---

*Frederic M. Thrasher, *The Gang* (Chicago: University of Chicago Press, 1936), pp. 94-95.

sometimes ruefully, sometimes with a touch of glee or even pride, that he is "just plain mean."

In describing what might be called the "spirit" of the delinquent culture, we have suggested also its *versatility*. Of the "antisocial" activities of the delinquent gangs, stealing, of course, looms largest. Stealing itself can be, and for the gang usually is, a diversified occupation. It may steal milk bottles, candy, fruit, pencils, sports equipment and cars; it may steal from drunks, homes, stores, schools and filling stations. No gang runs the whole gamut but neither is it likely to "specialize" as do many adult criminal gangs and "solitary" delinquents. More to our point, however, is the fact that stealing tends to go hand-in-hand with "other property offenses," "malicious mischief," "vandalism," "trespass," and truancy. This quality of versatility and the fusion of versatility and malice are manifest in the following quotation:

We would get some milk bottles in front of the grocery store and break them in somebody's hallway. Then we would break windows or get some garbage cans and throw them down someone's front stairs. After doing all this dirty work and running through alleys and yards, we'd go over to a grocery store. There, some of the boys would hide in a hallway while I would get a basket of grapes. When the man came after me, why the boys would jump out of their places and each grab a basket of grapes.*

Dozens of young offenders, after relating to the writer this delinquent episode and that, have summarized: "I

*Clifford R. Shaw and Henry D. McKay, *Social Factors in Juvenile Delinquency*, Vol. II of National Commission on Law Observance and Enforcement, *Report on the Causes of Crime* (Washington: U. S. Government Printing Office, 1931), p. 18.

guess we was just ornery." A generalized, diversified, protean "orneriness," not this or that specialized delinquent pursuit seems best to describe the vocation of the delinquent gang.[4]

Another characteristic of the subculture of the delinquent gang is *short-run hedonism*. There is little interest in long-run goals, in planning activities and budgeting time, or in activities involving knowledge and skills to be acquired only through practice, deliberation and study. The members of the gang typically congregate, with no specific activity in mind, at some street corner, candy store or other regular rendezvous. They "hang around," "roughhousing," "chewing the fat," and "waiting for something to turn up." They may respond impulsively to somebody's suggestion to play ball, go swimming, engage in some sort of mischief, or do something else that offers excitement. They do not take kindly to organized and supervised recreation, which subjects them to a regime of schedules and impersonal rules. They are impatient, impetuous and out for "fun," with little heed to the remoter gains and costs. It is to be noted that this short-run hedonism is not inherently delinquent and indeed it would be a serious error to think of the delinquent gang as dedicated solely to the cultivation of juvenile crime. Even in the most seriously delinquent gang only a small fraction of the "fun" is specifically and intrinsically delinquent. Furthermore, short-run hedonism is not characteristic of delinquent groups alone. On the contrary, it is common throughout the social class from which delinquents characteristically come. However, in the delinquent gang it reaches its finest flower. It is the fabric, as it were, of which delinquency is the most brilliant and spectacular thread.[5]

Another characteristic not peculiar to the delinquent gang but a conspicuous ingredient of its culture is an emphasis on *group autonomy,* or intolerance of restraint except from the informal pressures within the group itself. Relations with gang members tend to be intensely solidary and imperious. Relations with other groups tend to be indifferent, hostile or rebellious. Gang members are unusually resistant to the efforts of home, school and other agencies to regulate, not only their delinquent activities, but any activities carried on within the group, and to efforts to compete with the gang for the time and other resources of its members. It may be argued that the resistance of gang members to the authority of the home may not be a result of their membership in gangs but that membership in gangs, on the contrary, is a result of ineffective family supervision, the breakdown of parental authority and the hostility of the child toward the parents; in short, that the delinquent gang recruits members who have already achieved autonomy. Certainly a previous breakdown in family controls facilitates recruitment into delinquent gangs. But we are not speaking of the autonomy, the emancipation of *individuals.* It is not the individual delinquent but the gang that is autonomous. For many of our subcultural delinquents the claims of the home are very real and very compelling. The point is that the gang is a separate, distinct and often irresistible focus of attraction, loyalty and solidarity. The claims of the home versus the claims of the gang may present a real dilemma, and in such cases the breakdown of family controls is as much a casualty as a cause of gang membership.[6]

SOME ATTEMPTS AT EXPLANATION

THE LITERATURE on juvenile delinquency has seldom come to grips with the problem of accounting for the content and spirit of the delinquent subculture. To say that this content is "traditional" in certain areas and is "handed down" from generation to generation is but to state the problem rather than to offer a solution. Neither does the "social disorganization" theory[7] come to grips with the facts. This theory holds that the delinquent culture flourishes in the "interstitial areas" of our great cities. These are formerly "good" residential areas which have been invaded by industry and commerce, are no longer residentially attractive, and are inhabited by a heterogeneous, economically depressed and highly mobile population with no permanent stake in the community. These people lack the solidarity, the community spirit, the motivation and the residential stability necessary for organization, on a neighborhood basis, for the effective control of delinquency. To this argument we may make two answers. First, recent research has revealed that many, if not most, such "interstitial" and "slum" areas are by no means lacking in social organization. To the observer who has lived in them, many such areas are anything but the picture of chaos and heterogeneity which we find drawn in the older literature. We find, on the contrary, a vast and ramifying network of informal associations among like-minded people, not a horde of anonymous families and individuals, strangers to one another and rudely jostling one another in the struggle for existence. The social organization of the slum may lack the spirit and the objectives of organization in the "better" neighborhoods, but the slum is not necessarily a jungle. In the "delinquency area" as elsewhere, there is an awareness of community, an involvement of the individual in the lives and doings of the neighborhood, a concern about his reputation among his neighbors. The organization which exists may indeed not be adequate for the effective control of delinquency and for the solution of other social problems, but the qualities and defects of organization are not to be confused with the absence of organization.[8] However, granting the absence of community pressures and concerted action for the repression of delinquency, we are confronted by a second deficiency in this argument. It is wholly negative. It accounts for the presence of delinquency by the absence of effective constraints. If one is disposed to be delinquent, the absence of constraint will facilitate the expression of these impulses. It will not, however, account for the presence of these impulses. The social disorganization argument leaves open the question of the origin of the impulse, of the peculiar content and spirit of the delinquent subculture.

Another theory which has enjoyed some vogue is the "culture conflict" theory.[9] According to this view, these areas of high mobility and motley composition are lacking in cultural unity. The diverse ethnic and racial stocks have diverse and incongruent standards and codes, and these standards and codes are in turn inconsistent with those of the schools and other official representatives of the larger society. In this welter of conflicting cultures, the young person is confused and bedevilled. The adult world presents him with no clear-cut and authoritative models. Subject to a multitude of conflicting patterns, he respects none and assimilates none. He develops no respect for the legal order because it represents a culture which finds no support in his social world. He becomes delinquent.

From the recognition that there exists a certain measure of cultural diversity it is a large step to the conclusion that the boy is confronted by such a hodge-podge of definitions that he can form no clear conception of what is "right" and "wrong." It is true that some ethnic groups look more tolerantly on certain kinds of delinquency than others do; that some even encourage certain minor forms of delinquency such as picking up coal off railroad tracks; that respect for the courts and the police are less well established among some groups and that other cultural differences exist. Nonetheless, it is questionable that there is any ethnic or racial group which positively encourages or even condones stealing, vandalism, habitual truancy and the general negativism which characterizes the delinquent subculture. The existence of culture conflict must not be allowed to obscure the important measure of consensus which exists on the essential "wrongness" of these activities, except under special circumstances which are considered mitigating by this or that ethnic subculture. Furthermore, if we should grant that conflicting definitions leave important sectors of conduct morally undefined for the boy in the delinquency area, we must still explain why he fills the gap in the particular way he does. Like the social disorganization theory, the culture conflict theory is at best incomplete. The delinquent subculture is not a fund of blind, amoral, "natural" impulses which inevitably well up in the absence of a code of socially acquired inhibitions. It is itself a positive code with a definite if unconventional moral flavor, and it demands a positive explanation in its own right.

Another view which currently commands a good deal of respect we may call the "illicit means" theory.[10] According to this view our American culture, with its strongly democratic and equalitarian emphasis, indoctrinates all social classes impartially with a desire for high social status and a sense of ignominy attaching to low social status. The symbols of high status are to an extraordinary degree the possession and the conspicuous display of economic goods. There is therefore an unusually intense desire for economic goods diffused throughout our population to a degree unprecedented in other societies. However, the means and the opportunities for the legitimate achievement of these goals are distributed most unequally among the various segments of the population. Among those segments which have the least access to the legitimate channels of "upward mobility" there develop strong feelings of deprivation and frustration and strong incentives to find other means to the achievement of status and its symbols. Unable to attain their goals by lawful means, these disadvantaged segments of the population are under strong pressure to resort to crime, the only means available to them.

This argument is sociologically sophisticated and highly plausible as an explanation for adult professional crime and for the property delinquency of some older and semi-professional juvenile thieves. Unfortunately, it fails to account for the non-utilitarian quality of the subculture which we have described. Were the participant in the delinquent subculture merely employing illicit means to the end of acquiring economic goods, he would show more respect for the goods he has thus acquired. Furthermore, the destructiveness, the versatility, the zest and the wholesale negativism which characterizes the delinquent subculture are beyond the purview of this theory. None of the theories we have considered comes to grips with the data: the distinctive content of the delinquent subculture.

THE CLASS DISTRIBUTION OF THE DELINQUENT SUBCULTURE

WHO ARE the "carriers" of the delinquent subculture? Where in our social system is this subculture chiefly located? The answer must come largely from statistics compiled by police, courts and social agencies. These statistics, however, do not speak unequivocally. It is certain that those delinquencies which find their way into our permanent records are never more than a fraction of the total number of delinquencies. The statistics describe, in other words, *samples* of the total delinquent population, not that population itself, and the samples may sometimes be grossly unrepresentative. The ability to make sound inferences about the population from what we know about the samples depends upon experience with statistics in general and with the sources and methods of delinquency statistics in particular. At best our conclusions must often be tentative and uncertain.[11]

Apart from the hazards of delinquency statistics in general, we face another difficulty. These statistics do not differentiate delinquency which represents participation in the delinquent subculture which we have described from delinquency which does not. From the statistics on delinquency in general to inferences about the distribution of the delinquent subculture we must proceed with caution.

It is our conclusion, by no means novel or startling, that juvenile delinquency and the delinquent subculture in particular are overwhelmingly concentrated in the male, working-class sector of the juvenile population. This conclusion, however, has not gone unchallenged and it is so fundamental to the argument of this book that a review of the evidence is essential.

Almost all statistical analyses of juvenile delinquency agree that delinquency *in general* is predominantly a working-class phenomenon. It is logically conceivable, however, that the correlation between juvenile delinquency and social class is a statistical artifact produced by the biases of the police and the courts. Warner and Lunt, for example, in their study of "Yankee City," flatly state:

This disparity [of lower and upper class arrests] is not to be accounted for by the fact that "criminal behavior" is proportionately higher among lower-class juveniles or that there are more ethnic members whose children have been imperfectly adapted to Yankee City. It must be understood as a product of the amount of protection from outside interference that parents can give the members of their families.*

---

*W. Lloyd Warner and Paul S. Lunt, *The Social Life of a Modern Community* (New Haven: Yale University Press, 1941), p. 427.

Thrasher calls attention to the existence of delinquency in "overprivileged" as well as "underprivileged" communities.* Wattenberg's studies of *all* boys with whom the Detroit police deal, regardless of the history or disposition of the cases, "reveal that a surprisingly large number of offenders come from 'good' homes in 'good' neighborhoods."† Porterfield‡ had 337 college students, alleged not to be delinquent, indicate the frequency with which they had committed any of a list of 55 offenses. Every one of the students reported committing one or more of the offenses. Men reporting their pre-college offenses only averaged 17.6 offenses. These students were compared with a group of 2,049 children charged with delinquency in the Fort Worth juvenile court. These children, like any juvenile court sample, would represent the lower socioeconomic strata. For almost every offense, the percentage of college students reporting the offense exceeded the percentage of alleged delinquents charged with the offense.

That practically all children, regardless of social class, commit delinquencies is beyond dispute. Is there any need, however, to revise our conception that delinquency is most heavily concentrated in the working class? The statement of Warner and Lunt that there are no social class differences rests only on their claim that their inter-

---

*Frederic M. Thrasher, "Prevention of Delinquency in an Overprivileged Neighborhood," *Proceedings of the National Conference of Juvenile Agencies,* XL (April, 1944), pp. 96-106.

†William W. Wattenberg, "Boys Who Get in Trouble," *Journal of Education,* CXXXI (April, 1948), pp. 117-118.

‡Austin L. Porterfield, *Youth in Trouble,* (Austin: Leo Potishman Foundation, 1946).

views reveal this to be a fact but no published evidence is offered. Neither Wattenberg nor Thrasher, who are both serious students of juvenile delinquency, claim that their observations reverse the conclusions of most other research. Wattenberg (with Balistrieri) states, in another and more recent context: "It is assumed as amply demonstrated that in large American cities neighborhoods which have populations low in the socio-economic scale generally have high delinquency rates."* Porterfield's data demonstrate convincingly enough that the child who has never committed a delinquency is a rarity. They provide no basis, however, for comparing the relative frequency of delinquency *per child* in the different social levels. The college students were asked to report *all* the delinquencies they could remember in each of 55 offense categories. Furthermore, the list of 55 offenses presented to the college students is an extraordinarily comprehensive one, including, in addition to the more serious offenses, such transgressions as "shooting staples," "driving noisily by schools, churches," "prowling," "abusive language," and "loafing in a pool hall." Granted that such offenses as these may, under some circumstances, be adjudged delinquent by a juvenile court, the knowledge that the offense histories include all delinquencies of this order puts an average of 17.6 offenses per boy in a somewhat less startling and sinister light. The offenses of the juvenile court cases, on the other hand, are only those for which children were *charged in court* during

---

*William W. Wattenberg and James J. Balistrieri, "Gang Membership and Juvenile Misconduct," *American Sociological Review*, XV (December, 1950), 746.

the three years covered by the study. Most of these children, therefore, were represented in this study by only one or two cases. The study was not designed to reveal that portion of the iceberg which lay below the surface. Comparison between the college students and the court cases is, therefore, meaningless.

On the other hand, several careful large-scale studies which attempt to compensate for the inadequacies of official statistics tend to confirm the popular impression of the association between class and delinquency. Kvaraceus studied 761 cases of juveniles in the files of the Passaic Children's Bureau. These files are a reservoir of information on all children known to the police, the school, social and recreational agencies and other community agencies because of delinquent or "bothersome" behavior. Kvaraceus found: "One characteristic the overwhelming majority of the families of delinquent children in Passaic have in common. That characteristic is poverty."*

Schwarz analyzed data filed at a similar central register in the District of Columbia. Less than half of the cases were known to the juvenile court. It is generally assumed that such register data are more representative than court data, which are the result of a long selective process of complaint, arrest, arraignment and prosecution. It was found that the children from the higher income residential areas appeared relatively more frequently in the court cases

---

*William C. Kvaraceus, *Juvenile Delinquency and the School* (Yonkers-on-Hudson, N. Y.: World Book Company, 1945), p. 98. See also his "Juvenile Delinquency and Social Class," *Journal of Educational Sociology*, XVIII (September, 1944), 51-54.

than they did in the central register.* If any conclusion can be drawn from this, it is that the court cases *exaggerate* the proportion of delinquents from the upper social levels. Despite this, the official statistics invariably show an overwhelming concentration of delinquency in the working class areas.

The Cambridge-Somerville Youth Study bears, though only indirectly, on the representativeness of official statistics. A total of 114 "underprivileged" boys were studied from their eleventh to their sixteenth years by case workers enjoying their confidence. Of these 114, 101 had all been more or less serious juvenile offenders, but complaints were registered in court against only 40 of them. It was conservatively estimated that the total group had committed a minimum of 6,416 infractions of the law during the five-year period, but only 95 of these infractions became a matter of official complaint. If many delinquencies of upper-class children fail to find their way into the police and court records, the same is apparently true also of many delinquencies of working-class children, and conceivably even more true. The same study revealed that in the main, the transgressions of the official offenders were more frequent than those of the unofficial group, which suggests that the sample described by the official statistics tends to select the more serious offenders.†

---

*Edward E. Schwarz, "A Community Experiment in the Measurement of Juvenile Delinquency," in *Yearbook of the National Probation Association, 1945* (New York: National Probation Association, 1945), pp. 156-181.

†Fred J. Murphy, "Delinquency off the Record," in *Yearbook of the National Probation Association, 1946* (New York: National Probation Association, 1946), pp. 178-195.

We grant then, that delinquent behavior is by no means confined to the working-class level and that an adequate system of criminological theory must eventually cope with this fact.* It does not follow, however, that the popular impression that juvenile delinquency is primarily a product of working-class families and neighborhoods is an illusion. Egalitarian proclivities and sentimental humanitarianism dispose us to minimize the disproportionate concentration of delinquency among the less prosperous, powerful and respected. The lively concern of middle-class adults, into which category most of the readers of this volume fall, about the lapses of their own middle-class children dispose them to view with exceptional alarm and to magnify the volume of the delinquencies of the children of their own class. Nonetheless, the best evidence we have tends to support the traditional and popular conception of the distribution of juvenile delinquency in the class system.

We cannot assume, however, that all delinquency represents participation in the delinquent subculture. Is the delinquent subculture concentrated in the same manner as delinquency in general? There is no reason to think otherwise. It has been remarked that official statistics do not distinguish subcultural from other delinquency. Nonetheless, the conclusions of students who have been more specifically concerned with delinquency as a subculture tend also to localize subcultural delinquency in the lower socio-economic strata of our society. The principal conclusion of a monumental series of works by Shaw and McKay is that delinquency is a subcultural tradition in the areas

---

*See pages 157-169 below.

of the city inhabited by the lower socio-economic classes.

Although the "delinquent subculture" is not a category of delinquency statistics, there are a number of studies which distinguish group or gang delinquency from other delinquency. These studies furnish us with an important kind of evidence about the distribution of the delinquent subculture, for it is a hallmark of subcultural delinquency that it is acquired and practiced in groups rather than independently contrived by the individual as a solution to his private problems.

Thrasher, in his study of Chicago gangs—the culture-bearers *par excellence* of the delinquent subculture—found them overwhelmingly concentrated in the interstitial or slum areas of the city.* Hewitt and Jenkins examined 500 case records of problem children at the Michigan Child Guidance Institute for outstanding syndromes of problem behavior. They distinguished as "unsocialized aggressive" syndrome, a "socialized delinquency" syndrome, and an "overinhibited behavior" syndrome. The second of these is by definition delinquent and includes the characteristics "bad companions," "gang activities," "cooperative stealing," "furtive stealing," "truancy from home" and "staying out late nights." Of these characteristics, "cooperative stealing" appears to be the most diagnostic of the total syndrome. The "unsocialized aggressive" syndrome, while not necessarily delinquent, includes many delinquents, also, whose delinquent conduct, however, is not characteristically group activity. A variety of indices of socio-economic status show the "socialized delinquent"

---

*Frederic M. Thrasher, *op. cit.*, pp. 5-25.

children to be lower in status, on the average, than children of either of the other groups.* Wattenberg and Balistrieri found that gang delinquents were more likely than non-gang delinquents to "come from substandard homes and racially mixed neighborhoods, which at the time of this study in Detroit . . . tended to be less well-to-do. The non-gang group had a higher proportion of youngsters living in good neighborhoods."† These statistical studies tend to confirm the popular impression and the impression from a larger but statistically less precise literature that gang delinquency is primarily a working-class phenomenon.

THE SEX DISTRIBUTION OF THE DELINQUENT SUBCULTURE

THE SUBCULTURAL delinquency we have been talking about is overwhelmingly male delinquency. In the first place, delinquency *in general* is mostly male delinquency. Estimates of the exact ratio of female to male delinquency vary greatly. According to arrest data received by the Federal Bureau of Investigation, the ratio of girls' to boys' delinquency varies between one-seventh and one-nineteenth; according to juvenile court statistics received by the United States Children's Bureau, probably a more accurate index for our present purpose, it varies between one-fourth

---

*Lester E. Hewitt and Richard L. Jenkins, *Fundamental Patterns of Maladjustment* (published by The State of Illinois, no date), pp. 94, 97, 98, 104.

†William W. Wattenberg and James J. Balistrieri, *op. ct.*, p. 749.

and one-sixth.* Practically all published figures from these and other sources agree, however, on this: male delinquency is *at least* four times as common as female delinquency. It is probable that some types of offenses, when committed by girls, are less likely to be referred to the police and the courts and therefore less likely to find their way into our official statistics than when they are committed by boys. On the other hand, boys are less likely to be referred for certain types of offenses, notably sexual offenses. It is not probable that fuller and more accurate reporting of juvenile delinquency would change the direction of the numerical relationship between male and female delinquency.

Furthermore, wherever the literature compares male and female delinquency with respect to *kind,* rather than frequency only, it is the male delinquency which bears most conspicuously the earmarks of the delinquent subculture. One of these earmarks, it will be recalled, is diversity or versatility. It is not necessary here to belabor the reader with statistics. Authorities on delinquency are agreed that female delinquency, although it may appear euphemistically in the records as "ungovernability" or "running away" is mostly sex delinquency. Stealing, "other property offenses," "orneriness" and "hell-raising" in general are primarily practices of the male.† Even of sex

---

*Edward E. Schwarz, "Statistics of Juvenile Delinquency in the United States," *Annals of the American Academy of Political and Social Science,* CCLXI (January, 1939), p. 13.

†In this respect, the English statistics parallel our own. See Hermann Mannheim, "The Problem of Vandalism in Great Britain," *Federal Probation,* XIX (March, 1954), pp. 14-15 on the extraordinary contrast between boys and girls in the number of persons dealt with for malicious damage by the magistrates' courts.

delinquency the female has no monopoly. Were male participants in illicit heterosexual relations reported as frequently as their female partners, the richness and variety of male delinquency would be even more marked.

Again, the group or gang, the vehicle of the delinquent subculture and one of its statistically most manageable earmarks, is a boys' gang. For both sexes, the solitary delinquent is the exception rather than the rule.* However, in interpreting the significance of associates in delinquency, we must consider Kvaraceus' thoughtful observation:

The gang is largely a boys' institution. Among delinquent girls, one in three is a solitary delinquent, a figure not much different from that for boys. Another one third have committed their delinquencies with one companion, leaving one third only whose delinquencies are shared by two or more companions. Since the majority of delinquent girls, regardless of the "reason for referral," are in some degree sexually delinquent, the "number of companions" has a different connotation from what the same item has for boys, the episodes occuring with different boys at different times, except in the comparatively rare episodes of delinquent girls who have sex episodes with groups of boys in rapid sequence.†

As we might then expect, the proportion of delinquent episodes involving more than two participants is much greater among boys.

---

*See Norman Fenton, *The Delinquent Boy and the Correctional School,* (Claremont, California: Claremont Colleges Guidance Center, 1935), p. 79, for a summary of the studies on this subject. See also James S. Plant, "Who Is the Delinquent?" in *Forty-Seventh Yearbook of the National Society for the Study of Education,* Part I (Chicago: University of Chicago Press, 1935), p. 24 and William C. Kvaraceus, *Juvenile Delinquency and the School,* p. 116.

†William C. Kvaraceus, *op. cit.,* pp. 116-117.

Thrasher studied 1,313 gangs in the city of Chicago and concluded that, for practical purposes, girls do not form gangs. Not more than five or six of the 1,313 were gangs of girls and of these only one was clearly organized for delinquency.* Jenkins and Glickman analyzed data published by Ackerson for syndromes of problem behavior along the lines of the already cited study of Hewitt and Jenkins. As in the latter study, they distinguished a "socialized delinquent" syndrome for boys and another for girls. "Running with a gang" was prominent in the boys' "socialized delinquent" syndrome. However, ". . . there were so few entries of 'running with a gang' for girls that correlations were not computed for this trait."† Although we are primarily concerned with delinquency in the United States, we may observe that English studies suggest the same conclusions concerning the role of associates or gang membership.‡

The purpose of this discussion has not been to minimize the volume or significance of female delinquency, nor even to assert that female delinquency does not represent participation in a subculture. It is altogether conceivable that there is more than one delinquent subculture. If, however, female delinquents also have their subculture, it is a dif-

---

*Frederic M. Thrasher, *op. cit.*, pp. 228-229.

†Richard L. Jenkins and Sylvia Glickman, "Common Syndromes in Child Psychiatry," *American Journal of Orthopsychiatry*, XVI (April, 1946), 251.

‡Cyril Burt, *The Young Delinquent* (4th ed.; London: University of London Press, 1944), pp. 467-468; A. M. Carr-Saunders, Hermann Mannheim, and E. E. Rhodes, *Young Offenders: An Enquiry into Juvenile Delinquency* (Cambridge: Cambridge University Press, 1942), p. 111; J. H. Bagot, *Juvenile Delinquency* (London: Jonathan Cape, 1941), pp. 29, 59.

ferent one from that which we have described.* The latter belongs to the male role. It must be stressed that this book does not offer a theory to account for all delinquency in American society, nor even all male delinquency. It does, however, choose for its province that bloc of behavior which bulks largest in the total picture of juvenile crime.

---

*See pages 137-147 below.

CHAPTER III

A General Theory
of Subcultures

INTRODUCTION

THIS IS a chapter on subcultures in general, how they get started and what keeps them going. This seeming digression is really an integral part of our task. Any explanation of a particular event or phenomenon presupposes an underlying theory, a set of general rules or a model to which all events or phenomena of the same class are supposed to conform. Indeed, do we not mean by "explanation" a demonstration that the thing to be explained can be understood as a special case of the working out of such a set of general rules? For example, when we explain to a child why the rubber safety valve on a pressure cooker pops off when the interior of the cooker reaches a certain critical temperature, we first tell him that there are certain well-established relationships between pressure and temperature (which have been technically formulated in physics as Boyle's Law) and then we show him that the behavior of the valve is exactly what we should expect if the rules which describe those relationships are true. We do no more nor less when we explain the velocity of a falling body, the acquisition of a habit, an increase in the price of some commodity or the growth of a subculture. In every case, if the general theory which we invoke does not "fit" other phenomena of the same class, the explanation is not considered satisfactory. Thus, if *some* changes in the price level seem to be consistent with the "laws of supply and demand" but *other* changes in the price level are not, then the "laws" are considered unsatisfactory and *none* of the changes are explained by reference to these laws.

Therefore, it is appropriate that we set forth explicitly, if somewhat sketchily, the theory about subcultures in general that underlies our attempt to explain the delinquent subculture. If the explanation is sound, then the general theory should provide a key to the understanding of other subcultures as well. If the general theory does not fit other subcultures as well, then the explanation of this particular subculture is thrown into question.

ACTION IS PROBLEM-SOLVING

OUR POINT of departure is the "psychogenic" assumption that all human action—not delinquency alone—is an ongoing series of efforts to solve problems. By "problems" we do not only mean the worries and dilemmas that bring people to the psychiatrist and the psychological clinic. Whether or not to accept a proffered drink, which of two ties to buy, what to do about the unexpected guest or the "F" in algebra are problems too. They all involve, until they are resolved, a certain tension, a disequilibrium and a challenge. We hover between doing and not doing, doing this or doing that, doing it one way or doing it another. Each choice is an act, each act is a choice. Not every act is a *successful* solution, for our choice may leave us with unresolved tensions or generate new and unanticipated consequences which pose new problems, but it is at least an attempt at a solution. On the other hand, not every problem need imply distress, anxiety, bedevilment. Most problems are familiar and recurrent and we have at hand for them ready solutions, habitual modes of action which we have found efficacious and acceptable both to ourselves and to our neighbors. Other problems, however, are not so readily resolved. They persist, they nag, and they press for novel solutions.

What people do depends upon the problems they contend with. If we want to explain what people do, then we want to be clear about the nature of human problems and what produces them. As a first step, it is important to recognize that all the multifarious factors and circumstances that conspire to produce a problem come from one or the other of two sources, the actor's "frame of reference" and the "situation" he confronts. All problems arise and all problems are solved through changes in one or both of these classes of determinants.

First, the situation. This is the world we live in and where we are located in that world. It includes the physical setting within which we must operate, a finite supply of time and energy with which to accomplish our ends, and above all the habits, the expectations, the demands and the social organization of the people around us. Always our problems are what they are because the situation limits the things we can do and have and the conditions under which they are possible. It will not permit us to satisfy equally potent aspirations, *e.g.*, to enjoy the blessings of marriage and bachelorhood at the same time. The resources it offers may not be enough to "go around," *e.g.*, to send the children to college, to pay off the mortgage and to satisfy a thousand other longings. To some of us it may categorically deny the possibility of success, as we define success. To others, it may extend the possibility of success, but the only means which it provides may be morally repugnant; *e.g.*, cheating, chicanery and bootlicking may be the only road open to the coveted promotion.

But the niggardliness, the crabbiness, the inflexibility of the situation and the problems they imply are always relative to the actor. What the actor sees and how he feels about what he sees depend as much on his "point of view" as on the situation which he encounters. Americans do not see grasshoppers as belonging to the same category as pork chops, orange juice and cereal; other peoples do. Different Americans, confronting a "communist" or a "Negro," have very different ideas of what kind of person they are dealing with. The political office which one man sees as a job, another sees as an opportunity for public service and still another as something onerous and profitless to be avoided at all costs. Our beliefs about what is, what is possible and what consequences flow from what actions do not necessarily correspond to what is "objectively" true. "The facts" never simply stare us in the face. We see them always through a glass, and the glass consists of the interests, preconceptions, stereotypes and values we bring to the situation. This glass is our frame of reference. What is a "barrier" and what an "opportunity," what is a "reward" and what a "punishment," what is a "loss" and what a "gain" depends upon our goals and aspirations; they are not "given" by the bare facts of the situation taken by itself. Things are scarce or plentiful, hard or easy, precious or cheap depending upon our scale of values. Most important of all, perhaps, the moral insufficiency of this or that aspect of the situation, the moral obligation to "do something about it" and the moral impediments to quick and easy solutions derive not from the objective properties of the situation but from the moral standards within our frame of reference. Seen through one frame of reference the world is fraught with dark and frightening dilemmas; seen through another frame of reference, the "same" world is full of promise and cheer.

Our really hard problems are those for which we have no ready-at-hand solutions which will not leave us without feelings of tension, frustration, resentment, guilt, bitterness, anxiety or hopelessness. These feelings and therefore the inadequacy of the solutions are largely the result of the frame of reference through which we contemplate these solutions. It follows that an effective, really satisfying solution *must entail some change in that frame of reference itself.* The actor may give up pursuit of some goal which seems unattainable, but it is not a "solution" unless he can first persuade himself that the goal is, after all, not worth pursuing; in short, his values must change. He may resolve a problem of conflicting loyalties by persuading himself that the greater obligation attaches to one rather than to the other, but this too involves a change in his frame of reference: a commitment to some standard for adjudicating the claims of different loyalties. "Failure" can be transformed into something less humiliating by imputing to others fraud, malevolence or corruption, but this means adopting new perspectives for looking at others and oneself. He may continue to strive for goals hitherto unattainable by adopting more efficacious but "illicit" means; but, again, the solution is satisfying only to the degree that guilt is obviated by a change in moral standards. All these and other devices are familiar to us as the psychologist's and the psychoanalyst's "mechanisms of adjustment"—projection, rationalization, substitution, etc.—and they are all ways of coping with problems by a change within the actor's frame of reference.

A second factor we must recognize in building up a theory of subcultures is that human problems are not distributed in a random way among the roles that make up a social system. Each age, sex, racial and ethnic category, each occupation, economic stratum and social class consists of people who have been equipped by their society with frames of reference and confronted by their society with situations which are not equally characteristic of other roles. If the ingredients of which problems are compounded are likened to a deck of cards, your chances and mine of getting a certain hand are not the same but are strongly affected by where we happen to sit. The problems and preoccupations of men and women are different because they judge themselves and others judge them by different standards and because the means available to them for realizing their aspirations are different. It is obvious that opportunities for the achievement of power and prestige are not the same for people who start out at different positions in the class system; it is perhaps a bit less obvious that their levels of aspiration in these respects and therefore what it will take to satisfy them are likely also to differ. All of us must come to terms with the problems of growing old, but these problems are not the same for all of us. To consider but one facet, the decline of physical vigor may have very different meaning for a steel worker and a physician. There is a large and increasing scholarly literature, psychiatric and sociological, on the ways in which the structure of society generates, at each position within the system, characteristic combinations of personality and situation and therefore characteristic problems of adjustment.

Neither sociologists nor psychiatrists, however, have been sufficiently diligent in exploring the role of the social structure and the immediate social milieu in determining *the creation and selection of solutions.* A way of acting is never completely explained by describing, however convincingly, the problems of adjustment to which it is a response, *as long as there are conceivable alternative responses.* Different individuals *do* deal differently with the same or similar problems and these differences must likewise be accounted for. One man responds to a barrier on the route to his goal by redoubling his efforts. Another seeks for a more devious route to the same objective. Another succeeds in convincing himself that the game is not worth the candle. Still another accepts, but with ill grace and an abiding feeling of bitterness and frustration, the inevitability of failure. Here we shall explore some of the ways in which the fact that we are participants in a system of social interaction affects the ways in which we deal with our problems.

PRESSURES TOWARD CONFORMITY

IN A GENERAL way it is obvious that any solution that runs counter to the strong interests or moral sentiments of those around us invites punishment or the forfeiture of satisfactions which may be more distressing than the problem with which it was designed to cope. We seek, if possible, solutions which will settle old problems and not create new ones. A first requirement, then, of a wholly acceptable solution is that it be acceptable to those on whose cooperation and good will we are dependent. This immediately imposes sharp limits on the range of creativity and innovation. Our dependence upon our social milieu provides us with a strong incentive to select our solutions from among those already established and known to be congenial to our fellows.

More specifically, the consistency of our own conduct and of the frame of reference on which it is based with those of our fellows is a criterion of status and a badge of membership. Every one of us wants to be a member in good standing of some groups and roles. We all want to be recognized and respected as a full-fledged member of some age and sex category, as an American, perhaps also as a Catholic, a Democrat, a Southerner, a Yale man, a doctor, a man-of-the-world, a good citizen of West Burlap. For every such role there are certain kinds of action and belief which function, as truly and effectively as do uniforms, insignia and membership cards, as signs of membership. To the degree that we covet such membership, we are motivated to assume those signs, to incorporate them into our behavior and frame of reference. Many of our religious beliefs, esthetic standards, norms of speech, political doctrines, and canons of taste and etiquette are so motivated.

Not only recognition as members of some social category but also the respect in which others hold us are contingent upon the agreement of the beliefs we profess and the norms we observe with their norms and beliefs. However much we may speak of tolerance of diversity and respect for differences, we cannot help but evaluate others in terms of the measure of their agreement with ourselves. With people who think and feel as we do we are relaxed. We do not have to defend ourselves to them. We welcome them to our company and like to have them around. But in dissent there is necessarily implied criticism, and he who dissents, in matters the group considers important, inevitably alienates himself to some extent from the group and from satisfying social relationships.

Not only is consensus rewarded by acceptance, recognition and respect; it is probably the most important criterion of the *validity* of the frame of reference which motivates and justifies our conduct. The man who stands alone in holding something dear or in despising some good that others cherish, whether it be a style of art, a political belief, a vocational aspiration, or a way of making money not only suffers a loss of status; he is not likely to hold to his beliefs with much conviction. His beliefs will be uncertain, vacillating, unstable. If others do not question us, on the other hand, we are not likely to question ourselves. For any given individual, of course, some groups are more effective than others as authorities for defining the validity or plausibility of his beliefs. These are his "reference groups." For all of us, however, faith and reason alike are curiously prone to lead to conclusions already current in our reference groups. It is hard to convince ourselves that in cheating, joining the Christian Science Church, voting Republican or falsifying our age to buy beer we are doing the right thing if our reference groups are agreed that these things are wrong, stupid or ridiculous.[1]

We see then why, both on the levels of overt action and of the supporting frame of reference, there are powerful incentives not to deviate from the ways established in our groups. Should our problems be not capable of solution in ways acceptable to our groups and should they be sufficiently pressing, we are not so likely to strike out on our own as we are to shop around for a group with a different subculture, with a frame of reference we find more congenial. One fascinating aspect of the social process is the continual realignment of groups, the migration of individuals from one group to another in the unconscious quest for a social milieu favorable to the resolution of their problems of adjustment.

HOW SUBCULTURAL SOLUTIONS ARISE

NOW WE confront a dilemma and a paradox. We have seen how difficult it is for the individual to cut loose from the culture models in his milieu, how his dependence upon his fellows compels him to seek conformity and to avoid innovation. But these models and precedents which we call the surrounding culture are ways in which other people think and other people act, and these other people are likewise constrained by models in *their* milieux. *These models themselves, however, continually change.* How is it possible for cultural innovations to emerge while each of the participants in the culture is so powerfully motivated to conform to what is already established? This is the central theoretical problem of this book.

The crucial condition for the emergence of new cultural forms is the existence, *in effective interaction with one another, of a number of actors with similar problems of adjustment.* These may be the entire membership of a group or only certain members, similarly circumstanced, within the group. Among the conceivable solutions to their problems may be one which is not yet embodied in action and which does not therefore exist as a cultural model. This solution, except for the fact that is does not already carry the social criteria of validity and promise the social rewards of consensus, might well answer more neatly to the problems of this group and appeal to its members more effectively than any of the solutions already institutionalized. For each participant, this solution would be adjustive and adequately motivated provided that he could anticipate a simultaneous and corresponding transformation in the frames of reference of his fellows. Each would welcome a sign from the others that a new departure in this direction would receive approval and support. But how does one *know* whether a gesture toward innovation will strike a responsive and sympathetic chord in others or whether it will elicit hostility, ridicule and punishment? *Potential* concurrence is always problematical and innovation or the impulse to innovate a stimulus for anxiety.

The paradox is resolved when the innovation is broached in such a manner as to elicit from others reactions suggesting their receptivity; and when, at the same time, the innovation occurs by increments so small, tentative and ambiguous as to permit the actor to retreat, if the signs be unfavorable, without having become identified with an unpopular position. Perhaps all social actions have, in addition to their instrumental, communicative and expressive functions, this quality of being *exploratory gestures*. For the actor with problems of adjustment which cannot be resolved within the frame of reference of the established culture, each response of the other to what the actor says and does is a clue to the directions in which change may proceed further in a way congenial to the other and to the direction in which change will lack social support. And if the probing gesture is motivated by tensions common to other participants it is likely to initiate a process of *mutual* exploration and *joint* elaboration of a new solution. My exploratory gesture functions as a cue to you; your exploratory gesture as a cue to me. By a casual, semi-serious, noncommittal or tangential remark I may stick my neck out just a little way, but I will quickly withdraw it unless you, by some sign of affirmation, stick *yours* out. I will permit myself to become progressively committed but only as others, by some visible sign, become likewise committed. The final product, to which we are jointly committed, is likely to be a compromise formation of all the participants to what we may call a cultural process, a formation perhaps unanticipated by any of them. Each actor may contribute something directly to the growing product, but he may also contribute indirectly by encouraging others to advance, inducing them to retreat, and suggesting new avenues to be explored. The product cannot be ascribed to any one of the participants; it is a real "emergent" on a group level.

We may think of this process as one of mutual conversion. The important thing to remember is that we do not first convert ourselves and then others. The acceptability of an idea to oneself depends upon its acceptability to others. Converting the other is part of the process of converting oneself.

A simple but dramatic illustration may help. We all know that soldiers sometimes develop physical complaints with no underlying organic pathology. We know that these complaints, which the soldier himself is convinced are real, are solutions to problems. They enable the soldier to escape from a hazardous situation without feeling guilty or to displace his anxiety, whose true cause he is reluctant to acknowledge even to himself, upon something which is generally acknowledged to be a legitimate occasion for anxiety. Edward A. Strecker describes an episode of "mass psychoneurosis" in World War I. In a period of eight days, on a certain sector of the front, about 500 "gas casualties" reported for medical aid. There had been some desultory gas shelling but never of serious proportions.

Either following the explosion of a gas shell, or even without this preliminary, a soldier would give the alarm of "gas" to those in his vicinity. They would put on their masks, but in the course of a few hours a large percentage of this group would begin to drift into the dressing stations, complaining of indefinite symptoms. It was obvious upon examination that they were not really gassed.*

Strecker tells us that these symptoms were utilized as "a route to escape from an undesirable situation." What he does not tell us, but what seems extremely probable, is that for many and probably most of the soldiers, this route to escape was available only because hundreds of other soldiers were "in the same boat" and in continual communicative interaction before, during and after the shelling. One soldier might be ripe for this delusion but if his buddies are not similarly ripe he will have a hard time persuading them that he has been gassed, and if they persist in not being gassed he will have a hard time persuading himself. If all are ripe, they may, in a relatively short time, collectively fabricate a false but unshakeable belief that all have been gassed. It is most unlikely that these 500 soldiers would have been able to "describe all the details with convincing earnestness and generally some dramatic quality of expression" if they had not been able to communicate with one another and develop a common vocabulary

---

*Edward A. Strecker, *Beyond the Clinical Frontier* (New York: W. W. Norton and Company, 1940), pp. 77-78.

for interpreting whatever subjective states they did experience.

The literature on crowd behavior is another source of evidence of the ability of a propitious interaction situation to generate, in a short time, collective although necessarily ephemeral and unstable solutions to like problems. Students are agreed that the groundwork for violent and destructive mob behavior includes the prior existence of unresolved tensions and a period of "milling" during which a set of common sentiments is elaborated and reinforced. It is incorrect to assume, however, that a certain magic in numbers simply serves to lift the moral inhibitions to the expression of already established destructive urges. Kimball Young observes:

Almost all commentators have noted that individuals engaged in mass action, be it attack or panic flight, show an amazing lack of what are, under calmer conditions, considered proper morals. There is a release of moral inhibitions, social taboos are off, and the crowd enjoys a sense of freedom and unrestraint.*

He goes on to add, however:

Certainly those engaged in a pogrom, a lynching or a race riot have a great upsurge of moral feelings, the sense of righting some wrong . . . Though the acts performed may be viewed in retrospect as immoral, and may later induce a sense of shame, remorse and guilt, at the time they seem completely justified.†

It is true that ordinary moral restraints often cease to operate under mob conditions. These conditions do not, however, produce a suspension of all morality, a blind and amoral outburst of primitive passions. The action of

---

*Kimball Young, *Social Psychology* (2nd ed.; New York: F. S. Crofts and Company, 1946), p. 398.

†*Ibid.,* 399.

each member of the mob is in accordance with a collective solution which has been worked out during the brief history of the mob itself. This solution includes not only something to do but a positive morality to justify conduct at such gross variance with the mob members' ordinary conceptions of decency and humanity. In short, what occurs under conditions of mob interaction is not the annihilation of morality but a rapid transformation of the moral frame of reference.[2]

Here we have talked about bizarre and short-lived examples of group problem-solving. But the line between this sort of thing and large-scale social movements, with their elaborate and often respectable ideologies and programs, is tenuous. No fundamentally new principles have to be invoked to explain them.[3]

We quote from one more writer on the efficacy of the interaction situation in facilitating transformations of the frame of reference. The late Kurt Lewin, on the basis of his experience in attempts at guided social change, remarks:

... Experience in leadership training, in changing of food habits, work production, criminality, alcoholism, prejudices, all seem to indicate that it is usually easier to change individuals formed into a group than to change any one of them separately. As long as group values are unchanged the individual will resist changes more strongly the farther he is to depart from group standards. If the group standard itself is changed, the resistance which is due to the relationship between individual and group standard is eliminated.[*]

---

*Kurt Lewin, "Frontiers of Group Dynamics," *Human Relations,* I (June, 1947), 35.

The emergence of these "group standards" of this shared frame of reference, is the emergence of a new subculture. It is cultural because each actor's participation in this system of norms is influenced by his perception of the same norms in other actors. It is *sub*cultural because the norms are shared only among those actors who stand somehow to profit from them and who find in one another a sympathetic moral climate within which these norms may come to fruition and persist. In this fashion culture is continually being created, re-created and modified wherever individuals sense in one another like needs, generated by like circumstances, not shared generally in the larger social system. Once established, such a subcultural system may persist, but not by sheer inertia. It may achieve a life which outlasts that of the individuals who participated in its creation, but only so long as it continues to serve the needs of those who succeed its creators.

SUBCULTURAL SOLUTIONS TO STATUS PROBLEMS

ONE VARIANT of this cultural process interests us especially because it provides the model for our explanation of the delinquent subculture. Status problems are problems of achieving respect in the eyes of one's fellows. Our ability to achieve status depends upon the criteria of status applied by our fellows, that is, the standards or norms they go by in evaluating people. These criteria are an aspect of their cultural frames of reference. If we lack the characteristics or capacities which give status in terms of these criteria, we are beset by one of the most typical and yet distressing of human problems of adjustment. One solution is for individuals who share such problems to gravitate toward one another and jointly to establish new norms, new criteria of status which define as meritorious the characteristics they *do* posses, the kinds of conduct of which they *are* capable. It is clearly necessary for each participant, if the innovation is to solve his status problem, that these new criteria be shared with others, that the solution be a group and not a private solution. If he "goes it alone" he succeeds only in further estranging himself from his fellows. Such new status criteria would represent new subcultural values different from or even antithetical to those of the larger social system.

In general conformity with this pattern, social scientists have accounted for religious cults and sects such as the Oxford Group and Father Divine's Kingdom as attempts on the part of people who feel their status and self-respect threatened to create little societies whose criteria of personal goodness are such that those who participate can find surcease from certain kinds of status anxiety. They have explained such social movements as the Nazi Party as coalitions of groups whose status is unsatisfactory or precarious within the framework of the existing order and who find, in the ideology of the movement, reassurance of their importance and worth or the promise of a new society in which their importance and worth will be recognized. They have explained messianic and revivalistic religious movements among some American Indian and other non-literate groups as collective reactions to status problems which arise during the process of assimilation into a culture and social system dominated by white people. In this new social system the natives find themselves relegated to the lowest social strata. They respond by drawing closer together to one another and elaborating ideologies which emphasize the glories of the tribal past, the merit of membership in the tribe and an early millenium in which the ancient glory and dignity of the tribe will be reestablished.[4] All these movements may seem to have little in common with a gang of kids bent on theft and vandalism. It is true that they have little in common on the level of the concrete content of ideologies and value systems. In later chapters, however, we will try to show that the general principles of explanation which we have outlined here are applicable also to the culture of the delinquent gang.

SOME ACCOMPANIMENTS OF THE CULTURAL PROCESS

THE CONTINUED serviceability and therefore the viability of a subcultural solution entails the emergence of a certain amount of group solidarity and heightened interaction among the participants in the subculture. It is only in interaction with those who share his values that the actor finds social validation for his beliefs and social rewards for his way of life, and the continued existence of the group and friendly intercourse with its members become values for actor. Furthermore, to the extent that the new subculture invites the hostility of outsiders—one of the costs of subcultural solutions—the members of the subcultural group are motivated to look to one another for those goods and services, those relationships of cooperation and exchange which they once enjoyed with the world outside the group and which have now been withdrawn. This accentuates still further the separateness of the group, the dependence of the members on the group and the richness and individuality of its subculture. No group, of course, can live entirely unto itself. To some extent the group may be compelled to improvise new arrangements for obtaining services from the outside world. "The fix," for example, arises to provide for the underworld that protection which is afforded to legitimate business by the formal legal system and insurance companies.

Insofar as the new subculture represents a new status system sanctioning behavior tabooed or frowned upon by the larger society, the acquisition of status within the new group is accompanied by a loss of status outside the group. To the extent that the esteem of outsiders is a value to the members of the group, a new problem is engendered. To this problem the typical solution is to devalue the good will and respect of those whose good will and respect are forfeit anyway. The new subculture of the community of innovators comes to include hostile and contemptuous images of those groups whose enmity they have earned. Indeed, this repudiation of outsiders, necessary in order to protect oneself from feeling concerned about what they may think, may go so far as to make nonconformity with the expectations of the outsiders a positive criterion of status within the group. Certain kinds of conduct, that is, become reputable precisely because they are disreputable in the eyes of the "out-group."

One curious but not uncommon accompaniment of this process is what Fritz Redl has called "protective provocation." Certain kinds of behavior to which we are strongly inclined may encounter strong resistances because this behavior would do injury to the interests or feelings of people we care about. These same kinds of behavior would, however, be unequivocally motivated without complicating guilt feelings if those people stood to us in the relation of enemies rather than friends. In such a situation we may be unconsciously motivated to act precisely in those ways calculated to stimulate others to expressions of anger and hostility, which we may then seize upon as evidences of their essential enmity and ill will. We are then absolved of our moral obligations toward those persons and freer to act without ambivalence. The hostility of the "out-group," thus engendered or aggravated, may serve to protect the "in-group" from mixed feelings about its way of life.

CONCLUSION

OUR POINT of departure, we have said, is the psychogenic assumption that innovations, whether on the level of action or of the underlying frame of reference, arise out of problems of adjustment. In the psychogenic model, however, the innovation is independently contrived by the actor. The role of the social milieu in the genesis of the problem is recognized, but its role in the determination of the solution minimized. In the psychogenic model, the fact that others have problems similar to my own may lead them to contrive like solutions, but my problem-solving process runs to its conclusion unaffected by the parallel problem-solving processes of the others.

In the pure or extreme cultural-transmission model, on the other hand, the role of important differences in problems of adjustment and the motivation of newly acquired behavior by those problems tend to drop out of sight. Above all, the pure cultural-transmission view fails completely to explain the origin of new cultural patterns. Indeed, if the view we have proposed is correct, the cultural-transmission model fails to explain even the perpetuation of a cultural pattern through social transmission, for the recruitment of new culture-bearers presupposes life-problems which render them susceptible to the established pattern. The theory we have outlined, couched in terms of group problem-solving, attempts to integrate two views which, in the literature, frequently stand in presumed contrast to one another.

It is to be emphasized that the existence of problems of adjustment, even of like problems of adjustment among a plurality of actors, is not sufficient to insure the emergence of a subcultural solution. The existence of the necessary conditions for effective social interaction prerequisite to such a solution cannot be taken for granted. Who associates with whom is partly a matter of "shopping around" and finding kindred souls. But circumstances may limit this process of mutual gravitation of people with like problems and free and spontaneous communication among them. People with like problems may be so separated by barriers of physical space or social convention that the probability of mutual exploration and discovery is small. Free choice of associates may be regulated by persons in power, as parents may regulate the associates of their children. Where status differences among people with like problems are great, the probability of spontaneous comunication relating to private, intimate, emotionally involved matters is small. Where the problems themselves are of a peculiarly delicate, guilt-laden nature, like many problems arising in the area of sex, inhibitions on communication may be so powerful that persons with like problems may never reveal themselves to one another, although circumstances are otherwise favorable for mutual exploration. Or the problems themselves may be so infrequent and atypical that the probability of running into someone else whose interests would be served by a common solution is negligible.

Because of all these restraints and barriers to communication, as well as the costs of participation in subcultural groups, which may sometimes be counted excessive, subcultural solutions may not emerge, or particular individuals may not participate in them. Nonetheless, the problems of adjustment may be sufficiently intense and persistent that they still press for some kind of change that will mitigate or resolve the problem. Since group solutions are precluded, the problem-solving may well take a "private," "personal-social" or "neurotic" direction and be capable of satisfactory description in primarily psychogenic terms.

A complete theory of subcultural differentiation would state more precisely the conditions under which subcultures emerge and fail to emerge, and would state operations for predicting the content of subcultural solutions. Such a task is beyond the scope of this chapter, and, in any case, the completion of this theory must await a great deal more of hard thinking and research. In this chapter we have tried to put on the record, in a highly general and schematic way, the basic theoretical assumptions which underlie the chapters which are to follow. In these chapters, in conformity with the model we have proposed, we shall try to demonstrate that certain problems of adjustment tend, in consequence of the structure of American society, to occur most typically in those role sectors where the delinquent subculture is endemic. Then we shall try to show how the delinquent subculture provides a solution appropriate to those particular problems and to elaboration and perpetuation by social groups.

CHAPTER IV

Growing Up
in a Class System

THE FAMILY IS NOT THE WORLD

THE DELINQUENT subculture is mostly to be found in the working class. It does not follow that working-class children are necessarily more beset with problems of adjustment than are middle-class children. It has been plausibly argued by some students of social class in America that growing up in the middle class is, on the whole, a more frustrating experience than growing up in the working class. But the problems may be different and to different problems the conceivable alternative solutions may be different. The range of alternatives may be further narrowed and the ultimate solution more completely determined by other circumstances which vary with social class, such as the conditions of communication and association, the facilities at one's disposal and other interests and values which might be jeopardized by certain of the solutions. It will not be our task, then, to show that the working-class male child has problems. It will be our task to show that the *kinds* of problems which he has and the context in which they exist are adequate to motivate the subculture we have described.[1]

We shall not attempt to catalog, in the manner of a clinician interpreting the behavior of a patient, all of the problems which may confront children and which may condition the probability, the extent and the manner of their participation in the delinquent culture. Every child, and for that matter every human being, is the hub or nexus of a unique arrangement of circumstances and consequently of a unique constellation of problems. To understand fully the behavior of a particular child, the proper task of the psychologist, it is necessary to take this uniqueness fully into account. To account for the salient characteristics of a culture pattern, however, characteristics which repeat themselves in thousands of little collectivities widely scattered in time and space and which persist while generations of participants come and go, it is necessary to seek for common problems and for common ground for joint participation in a common solution. In our inquiry into the circumstances of the working-class child which might be capable of generating this subculture, we shall be especially concerned with those which are typical, recurrent and shared.

In our treatment of the family also, our emphases shall differ from those most typical of the clinician's and the psychologist's case studies. In trying to account for "problem" behavior, these case studies typically put the child in the context of his family and trace, with great subtlety and detail, the evolution of his relationships with his parents and siblings. Depending upon his theoretical leanings, the analyst or case worker will emphasize this or that aspect of this complex system of relationships. What is important for our purposes, however, is his tendency to assume that, by and large, the behavior of the child can be accounted for in terms of the *internal structure* of this little social system without reference to the larger social system within which it is embedded. That is to say, he tends to assume that the sources of the child's personality, his life problems and the circumstances that determine their solutions are to be found within the family, that behavior within and without the family is an expression of impulses formed altogether within the family.

Our own approach in no way minimizes the role of the family; if anything, it magnifies it. We emphasize, however, the ways in which consequences of family membership depend upon the social world outside the family. We emphasize, first, that the very fact of membership in a particular family, quite apart from the child's experiences within the family, has meaning to the child. Families are not merely networks of social relationships which have consequences for the personalities of their members. Like ball clubs, lodges, churches, ladies' aid societies, boy scout troops and college fraternities, they are recognized social units, designated by names which distinguish them from other units of the same general class and possessed of position, privileges, reputation and status of their own. Membership in such a unit or collectivity means that one shares with the other members a common name, a common iden- tification and a common status; that, for certain purposes or in certain contexts, he is treated not as an individual with a unique personality but as a member and repre- sentative of the group. In some societies family member- ship, in conjunction with age and sex, completely over- shadows any other characteristics, whether group member- ships or personal traits and conduct, in regulating the behavior of members of different families. The situation is akin to the encounter of two soldiers of opposing sides, of two members of opposing football teams. The identifica- tion of the opposite number's group membership suffices to determine one's attitudes and conduct toward him. To some degree such categorical treatment of others simply as members of families exists in all societies. To some de- gree, therefore, *the position of the family in the social structure,* particularly its status vis-a-vis other families, determines the experiences and the problems which all members of the family will encounter in their dealings with the world outside the family.

The other difference in emphasis concerns the relation- ship between the child's experiences within the family, especially the impact of the family upon the personality of the child, and his experiences in the world outside the family. We have suggested that the clinician is typically prone to treat the world outside as a theatre in which the child acts out the roles and gives expression to the impulses formed within the family. But the world outside may be more properly likened to an arena than a theatre. It consists of ineluctable facts, persons and activities, challenges and responses as objective and autonomous as the facts within the family. They are not props for a play, but real prizes, real barriers and real deprivations able, in their own right, to gratify, to frustrate and to leave their print on the developing personality.

This is not to suggest that the world within and the world without the family are so segregated that what happens in the one has nothing to do with what happens to the other. They are rather continuous and even interpenetrating fields within a common life-space, and events anywhere in this life-space help to determine events anywhere else and to color their emotional significance. Thus the family, directly through its supervisory activities and indirectly through its influence on the interests and preferences of the child, helps to determine the kinds of people and situations he will encounter outside. His experiences in the family are the most important determinants of the frame of reference through which the child perceives, interprets and evaluates the world outside. And the knowledge, habits and skills which he acquires in the home help to determine his capacity for dealing successfully with situations outside. But still the child, when he steps outside the home, like the high school graduate when he seeks his first job, must meet the world on its own terms. In our own inquiry, then, we shall be much concerned with what happens to the child in the family, but in order to appreciate the importance of what happens there we shall have to be concerned as well with the opportunities and barriers, the challenges and expectations in a wider social milieu.

FAMILIES ARE UNITS IN A CLASS SYSTEM

WHEN WE view the family as a collectivity, membership in which confers upon its members a certain status in the wider society, we are treating the family as a unit in a social class system.[2] The word "social class" is in bad odor in American society. We prefer to think that the social classes, whatever they are, do not exist in the United States. Let us make clear what we mean by social class in this book. If a citizen of your community is presented with a list of families known to him and asked to arrange them in order of "social standing," "position," "rank," or "reputation" in that community, with the understanding that a number of families might occupy approximately the same position on the scale, he will probably be able to do so without too much difficulty. If several citizens are asked to do the same, they may produce somewhat divergent results, but on the whole they are likely to exhibit remarkable agreement. Put otherwise, in any community there is likely to be a high degree of consensus that certain families are "good families," "fine old families," families "high in society"; that other families are "low class" families, "no-count" families, families with "no standing" in the community; and that other families fall somewhere in between, "poor but honest" families, "good, solid working-class" families, "respectable middle-class" families. We say this is so because substantially the procedure we have suggested has been followed numerous times in sociological research and consistently yielded these results. For our purposes, this arrangement of families in order of relative rank or standing in the community is the community's social class system.

To say that every community has a social class system is not to say that the system is the same in all communities, even within the United States. The things that people go by in rating or evaluating families—more technically, the "criteria of social class status"—are not everywhere accorded the same weight. Among the most important criteria we find lineage, or the social class status of the family's forbears, the length of time the family has been established in the community, wealth or possessions, ethnic origin, style of living, public service, and the husband's job. Not each of these is of the same importance in all communities, although there is general agreement among students of social class that, by and large, in American society the prestige of the husband's job "swings more weight" than any other criterion.

Communities may differ also with respect to the way in which families are distributed along this spectrum; the proportion of families at the one or the other extreme or within some range in between may vary. Communities may differ with respect to the sharpness of the breaks, that is, the discontinuity of the groupings in the spectrum. In one community there may be two or three distinct status groupings, and any family may be easily placed in one or another of these generally recognized "classes." In another community, there may be a continuous gradation of status with no sharp breaks or barriers defining two, four, six or some other number of clearly distinct classes. Finally, communities may differ with respect to the ease and the frequency of movement from one status level to another, or "vertical social mobility."

For our present purposes, however, these differences are secondary. The important thing is that in all American communities one's family enjoys a certain status, high or low, vis-a-vis other families, and that the status of one's family is one of the main determinants of the respect, the deference and the power a person commands. It is a matter of common observation that in certain respects husband and wife, at least, tend to be treated as social equals. If I am good enough to be invited to your home, or to your daughter's wedding, then so is my wife; and if my wife is good enough, then so am I. I cannot climb successfully— or fail—without my family sharing in my fortune. This is more than merely a matter of their participation in my earnings. Not only am I the responsible "provider" for their materials needs, the one who "brings home the bacon," but the respect that attaches to my job attaches to my wife and children severally.

Of course Americans do not as a rule show their consciousness of social class position by bowing and scraping or arrogantly demanding an elaborate display of deference. The "etiquette of deference in a democracy"[3] forbids the manifest and explicit acknowledgement of status differences. Status consciousness is nonetheless clearly and unmistakably manifested whenever we admit some people but not "just anybody" to familiar, informal "primary group relations," or seek to be accepted by others to such relations. For mutual acceptance on such terms is an acknowledgement of status equality. We speak here of sitting at the same family dinner, of relaxing in the same living room, of belonging to the same clubs and cliques, of mingling naturally and easily at the same cocktail parties, of playing poker, bridge or golf together, of exchanging gifts, of going to the movies together, of "dropping in" uninvited, of dating and marrying. Granting and withholding such relationships speaks softly but eloquently of social acceptance and social distance. These relationships are not exclusively based on social class status position—that is, on status which one enjoys by virture of membership in a particular family—but they are so bound up with family considerations that students of social class have found the analysis of these patterns of informal association in a community one of the most useful keys to the discovery of its class system.

How about our children? To what degree are they conversant with this social class system and participants in its workings? It would be rash to speak glibly in the present state of our knowledge. We do know that children, in increasing measure as they grow older, sort themselves, in school and out, into cliques corresponding to the social class positions of their families. Of this we will speak more in a later section. However, it does not necessarily follow that this selective association, which has been established beyond cavil, is primarily a result of the children's perceptions of the class status of their families. To some degree it is certainly the result of the perception of *personal characteristics* which happen to be correlated with social class.

We need more research on the extent to which children respond to themselves and to one another as members of families rather than as individuals. However, we do know that as the child's sense of self emerges, as his name—"Frank" or "Sheldon" or "Karl"—acquires the capacity to evoke an image which he identifies as "I" and "me" and about which he feels pride and shame, his membership in a particular family whose members share the common symbol "Smith" or "Brown" or "Donahue" becomes an integral part of the self. His attitudes toward himself, his self-respect, his "ego-involvement" become bound up with the sentiments, the prestige or the ignominy that cling to the family name or to any member of the family. "My father can lick your father" is an early and naive manifestation of this identification and ego-involvement, as are his reactions to aspersions on his mother's good name or his pride in the uniform and bearing of his brother in the service. It takes a long time for him to progress from this stage to the point where he can place his own family and others in the prestige continuum in the same way that adults do. But his family, consciously and unconsciously, does what it can to help. The child observes his parents and others interact with the janitor, the plumber, the doctor, the insurance agent, the bank clerk, the social worker, the teacher, the landlord. He learns to make the distinctions adults make, to apply the criteria they apply and to evaluate their families and his own family relative to theirs, as the adults do. He learns also to recognize and to value the signs of membership in a social class: clothing and equipment, homes, neighborhood and cars. By the time he is eleven or twelve years old his knowledge of the class system has grown quite sophisticated. His estimates of his school classmates as "high-in-society," "low-in-societ "in-between" show impressive, although as yet imp agreement with the judgments af adults. Celia B. Stendler, in one of our most valuable studies of this subject, observes that:

Sixth and eighth graders correctly associated many symbols with a particular class. They knew that the class to which one belonged was indicated by the kind of job, family and home one had, and the section of town in which one lived. Eighth graders were very specific in their comments, and many of the reasons disclosed very subtle class distinctions.*

The child learns also from his parents, often under protest from the child, that there are children with whom it is well to play and others with whom one does not play, children whom one does and others whom one does not bring to the house, those with whom his parents like to see him go camping, swimming or on parties and those who are tabooed. In varying degrees in different families and in different social levels, his parents show their approval and disapproval of his associates and try to regulate them. Partly, and probably for the most part, this discrimination by his parents is clearly based on personal characteristics of the children concerned. Partly, however, it is categorical, independent of knowledge of personal characteristics and based on generalized attitudes toward their families. Much of this purposive control may be obviated by the simple device of living in a part of town where acceptable associates are the only ones available. But occasional active intervention by the parents is almost always necessary, and this

---

*Celia B. Stendler, *Children of Brasstown* (Urbana: University of Illinois, 1949), p. 71

intervention serves the function of underscoring the lines that distinguish the various degrees of social acceptability. At the same time the child is also at the receiving end, noting that he is welcomed by some and rebuffed by others. Whatever the psychological processes or consequences involved in this learning process, the child is learning to make the distinctions the adults about him make, although his readiness to select and discriminate on the basis of these distinctions probably lags behind his intellectual apprehension of them.

JUDGING OUR CHILDREN: THE MIDDLE-CLASS MEASURING ROD

THE READER may feel that this picture is overdrawn, that it grossly distorts the fundamentally democratic social relations of American society. Do not Americans believe and try to teach their children to believe that people should be judged only on the basis of their character, achievements and personality, that labels signifying background, group affiliation or ancestry but which tell us nothing about the *person* are not a legitimate basis for judging people?

The answer, of course, is "Yes." Democracy, in this sense of the word, is not a fiction. The status which the child enjoys by virtue of his membership in a recognized kinship unit is but one determinant of his respect, his power, his social acceptability. The very fact that we acknowledge grudgingly, if at all, that family membership operates to determine status, suggests that there are important competing standards for judgment as well.

Let us turn, however, to the more "democratic" mode of

judgment or evaluation. The child in America is undoubt-edly evaluated, to a greater degree than in most other societies, as an individual. But this does not take us out of the realm of invidious status distinctions. It takes us, rather, to a consideration of another status system, one in which children of different social levels may be and are directly compared in terms of the same set of "achieved" criteria. In this status system children of any social class may compete with one another and in this sense it is democratic. The cards are not dealt and the hands all played for him before the child appears on the scene. How-ever, this democracy has certain important implications. To the degree that ancestry as such is scrupulously ignored, it means that any child may be legitimately compared, to his advantage or his loss, with any other child of the same age and sex. The child's "status universe," the people against whom he is measured and against whom he mea-sures himself, is enormously extended. In "undemocratic" feudal and peasant societies, it is assumed that society is permanently divided into natural social divisions or orders. Corresponding to each of these orders is a different set of expectations or standards for evaluation of persons. The child of a peasant family is not "ego-involved" in his dif-ferences from the landlord's son. They are in different status universes.[4]

In a society like ours, however, in which a child may be legitimately compared, *in terms of the same criteria,* with "all comers" regardless of family background, it does not follow that the ability to achieve these criteria is neces-sarily distributed without regard to family background and social class. Systematic class-linked differences in the ability to achieve will relegate to the bottom of the status pyramid those children belonging to the most disadvantaged classes, not by virtue of their class position as such but by virtue of their lack of the requisite personal qualifications resulting from their class-linked handicaps. In short, where opportunities for achievement are class-linked, status discontent will be generated to the degree that the status system is democratic, to the degree that the status universe is maximized. It becomes necessary for us, then, to consider the criteria for the evaluation of children in American society and whether the capacity to achieve in terms of those criteria is conditioned by social class position.

There is more than one set of non-ascriptive criteria for differential evaluation of children in our society, and these criteria carry different weight in the different social levels. We run some danger, then, of oversimplification, and must take care to specify that the norms we shall describe here are most clearly exemplified and applied by what we shall loosely call "middle-class" in contrast to "working-class" people, that is, by middle-class parents, teachers, social workers, ministers and church workers, by the adults sponsoring and managing settlement houses, Boy Scout troops, and other agencies for organized and supervised recreation, and, to a considerable extent, by middle-class children. Whether these norms are applied by working-class children or not, these children cannot be indifferent to them. They are the norms of the people who *run things* in politics, business, religion and education. They are the norms of the distinguished people who symbolize and represent the local and national communities with which the children identify. Furthermore, even though these norms have a more tenuous footing in the working class than the middle class, they are the norms also of many of the children's own working-class neighbors. For, wherever we draw the lines between the working class and the middle class in economic or occupational terms, the resulting groupings will not be internally homogeneous with respect to cultural beliefs and values. Many working-class people will resemble middle-class people with respect to their criteria for evaluating children and indeed, it is probable that *most* working-class Americans are to some degree under the spell of this particular set of norms. Though we refer to them here, then, as "middle-class" norms, they are really manifestations of the dominant American value system and even working-class children must come to terms with them.

These norms are, in effect, a tempered version of the Protestant ethic[5] which has played such an important part in the shaping of American character and American society. In brief summary, this middle-class ethic prescribes an obligation to strive, by dint of rational, ascetic, self-disciplined and independent activity, to achieve in worldly affairs. A not irrebuttable but common corollary is the presumption that "success" is itself a sign of the exercise of these moral qualities.

From another point of view, these middle-class standards may be regarded as the positive evaluation in children of those characteristics which facilitate and lay the ground for the achievement of respectable social class status in adulthood. From this point of view, there is an important continuity and integration of the legitimate expectations attaching to childhood and adult roles, in the sense that indoctrination with this morality prepares the child for the easy assumption of, or success in, the adult roles.

One more observation is here in order. The requisites for the achievement of social class status in the adult role are not quite the same for men and for women. The social class status of both men and women is that of their family. The status of the family, in turn, depends, more than it does on any other one thing, on the occupational achievement of the male "head." The social class status of women depends primarily upon marriage to an occupationally successful male. The road to vertical mobility for men, much more than for women, then, is through independent occupational achievement. To the extent that middle-class standards for the evaluation of children are continuous with adult roles, we should expect these standards to be different, at least in emphasis, for boys and girls. The following summary description[6] of these middle-class standards is primarily applicable to the male role.

1. Ambition is a virtue; its absence is a defect and a sign of maladjustment. Ambition means a high level of aspiration, aspiration for goals difficult of achievement. It means also an orientation to long-run goals and long-deferred rewards. It means an early determination to "get ahead." It is incumbent upon the good parent to encourage in his children those habits and goals which will help them to be "better off" than himself, and his first duty is to make his child *want* to "be somebody."

2. The middle-class ethic is an ethic of individual responsibility. It applauds resourcefulness and self-reliance, a reluctance to turn to others for help. In Margaret Mead's words:

Parenthood in America has become a very special thing and parents see themselves not as giving their children final status and place, rooting them firmly for life in a dependable social structure, but merely as training them for a race which they will run alone.*

Although it recognizes, as does the ethic of every society, a certain virtue in generosity, it minimizes the obligation to share with others, even with one's own kin, especially insofar as this obligation is likely to interfere with the achievement of one's own goals. If one's first obligation is to help, spontaneously and unstintingly, friends and kinsmen in distress, a kind of minimum security is provided for all, but nobody is likely to get very far ahead of the game.

3. Middle-class norms place a high evaluation on the cultivation and possession of skills and on the tangible achievements which are presumed to witness to the possession of skills and the application of effort. Outstanding performance of almost any kind is applauded, *e.g.*, athletic achievement, but there is special emphasis on academic achievement and the acquisition of skills of potential economic and occupational value.

4. Middle-class norms place great value on "worldly asceticism," a readiness and an ability to postpone and to subordinate the temptations of immediate satisfactions and self-indulgence in the interest of the achievement of long-

*Margaret Mead, *And Keep Your Powder Dry* (New York: William Morrow and Company, 1942), p. 75.

run goals. Industry and thrift, even divorced from any conscious utilitarian objectives, are admirable in themselves.

5. Rationality is highly valued, in the sense of the exercise of forethought, conscious planning, the budgeting of time, and the allocation of resources in the most economic and technologically most efficient way. This involves a disinclination to trust to the irrational workings of chance and moral suspiciousness of gambling despite the fact that gambling enjoys a certain shady popularity among many middle-class adults and children.

6. The middle-class value system rewards and encourages the rational cultivation of manners, courtesy and personability. In the middle-class world, mastery of certain conventions of speech and gesture carry prestige and are instrumental to success. Furthermore, and more importantly, the middle-class adult, especially the male, circulates in a world of numerous transient and segmental but highly important secondary-group relationships. A facility in such relationships, an ability to "make friends and influence people," or at least to avoid antagonizing them is vital. A pamphlet published by the National Association of Manufacturers for free distribution to school children and significantly entitled *Your Future is What You Make It* neatly expresses this theme:

Here's an item for your personal rule book: *Don't let your courtesy get rusty.* You'll have to get along with all the people around you, so treat them as you wish to be treated. In any organization, there's a certain amount of friction. No wonder we prize those persons who make life happier by helping to reduce it! *Getting along with people is one of the most impor-*

*tant requirements for those who want to get ahead on the job—
or off.**

The achievement of these skills necessarily implies the cultivation of patience, self-control and the inhibition of spontaneity.

7. The middle-class ethic emphasizes the control of phys-cal aggression and violence, which are subversive, on the ɔne hand, of good personal relations with as many people as possible and, on the other hand, of an impersonal competitive order in which intellectual, technical and social skills may realize their maximum value.

8. Recreation should be "wholesome." That is, one should not "waste" time but spend his leisure "constructively." Play is necessary and desirable, but play gains in merit to the degree that it involves some measure of foresight, study, practice and sustained endeavor toward the development of a collection, a skill or a fund of specialized knowledge. Hence the pride and pleasure of the middle-class parent in his children's pursuit of a "hobby."

9. Lastly, middle-class values emphasize "respect for property." This does not mean a desire for material goods nor does it mean simple "honesty." It means a particular cluster of attitudes regarding the nature of property rights and the significance of property.

It includes an emphasis on the *right* of the owner to do as he wishes with his belongings *versus* an emphasis on the *claims* of others who may stand in primary-group relationships to the owner. It includes an emphasis on the explicit

---

*Your Future is What You Make It (New York: National Association of Manufacturers, 1947), pp. 23-24.

consent of the owner prior to the use or conversion of his articles of property *versus* "helping yourself" with the understanding that the willingness and the obligation to share is implicit in your relationship to the owner. It includes a quasi-sacred attitude toward things, whether others' or one's own or collective property. Things are to be husbanded, treated carefully, not wantonly wasted, carelessly abused or destroyed.

The orderly functioning of the middle-class economic world depends upon a system of strict property accounting, the clear and precise allocation of property rights to individuals or the incumbents of certain offices, and the transfer of rights to access, control and usufruct in accordance with fixed and formal procedures, either an explicit act of giving, a decree or order by a duly authorized official or an act of contract. Casualness and imprecision in the allocation and delimitation of property rights and failure to signalize changes in these rights by written instrument or explicit verbal understandings are a source of confusion and conflict in the world of commerce and large-scale organization. Children, it is felt, should get into the habit of thinking in these terms.

Another source of this stress on respect for property lies in the ethic of individual responsibility. This means that a person should make his own way in the world by dint of his own efforts. His claims on the resources accumulated by others and their claims on his resources are minimized. Such claims still exist, particularly between close kin and friends, but they are more severely limited than in most cultures. Insofar as giving and sharing are approved ("Don't be selfish; let your little brother play with your toys!") the emphasis tends to be placed on the merit of the giver rather than on the right of the recipient.

Property, furthermore, is not only of utilitarian or esthetic value, but it is extraordinarily ego-involved, for it is the most conspicuous sign of achievement, the most universally legible symbol of worth. All property, including cash, is, in this sense, of purely sentimental value. But it is of little value in this symbolic respect if it may be easily dissipated by either oneself or others. The ability of property to perform this function is not incompatible with sharing, provided that the claims of the other are not pressed as a matter of legitimate expectation. If things are explicitly given without being asked for or in response to a properly respectful request, the whole transaction becomes a minor ritual dramatizing the ownership and the act of supererogation. Daddy solemnly requests a loan of Johnny. Sister is justly angry because somebody used her stationery without asking, although sister would have been delighted to share it if the other "had only asked." The visitor to the middle-class home is careful to write his bread-and-butter letter.

Lastly, a middle-class home is, to a great extent, a carefully ordered museum of artifacts for display, representing a great deal of "congealed labor." Their function for conspicuous consumption depends upon the preservation of their original state and upon ready recognition of their value, and middle-class children are trained to respect such objects and the order in which they have been lovingly arranged.

SOCIAL CLASSES AS CULTURAL SETTINGS

THE ABILITY to conform to these norms and therefore to achieve status in these terms does not depend upon a simple effort of will. Conformity comes easily when the child has internalized these norms because he has grown up in a world in which example, precept and reward have always emphasized them and when training has equipped him with the necessary skills and habits. It comes hard when his world of adult intimates does not so consistently exemplify these values or inculcate the necessary skills. The middle-class home is more likely to train the child to compete successfully for status in terms of these norms than is the working-class home.

In speaking of cultural differences between middle-class and working-class society, we do not mean to imply that there are two sharply demarcated and culturally homogeneous classes. In most American communities these categories merge insensibly and the families included in either one are heterogeneous indeed. Some of our best examples of "middle-class culture" are to be found in "upwardly mobile" working-class families. W. Lloyd Warner* distinguishes a lower-lower and an upper-lower class, but each of these is culturally heterogeneous. E. Wight Bakke's† and Allison Davis'‡ descriptions of working-class culture

---

*W. Lloyd Warner and Paul S. Lunt, *The Social Life of a Modern Community* (New Haven: Yale University Press, 1941).

†E. Wight Bakke, *The Unemployed Worker* (New Haven: Yale University Press, 1940).

‡Allison Davis, "The Motivation of the Underprivileged Worker," in William F. Whyte (ed.), *Industry and Society* (New York: McGraw-Hill Book Company, 1946).

differ markedly in emphasis. Bakke's working people are, on the whole, a couple of notches "higher" than those Davis describes. When we speak of "working-class culture" in the following pages, we shall be speaking of cultural characteristics and emphases which by no means characterize all working-class families but which do tend, in a gross statistical sense, to distinguish the cultural milieu of the working-class boy from that of the middle-class boy, and particularly which tend to characterize the least esteemed and economically most insecure levels of the working class. There is now a fairly abundant literature on this subject of class differences in culture and child rearing.[7] The following discussion summarizes those differences most relevant to the acquisition of prowess in the contest for status.

Both in preachment and in practice the working-class boy is likely to find the middle-class ethic much attenuated in the lives of his parents and the parents of his neighborbood peers. Their aspirations with respect to jobs and income are likely to be well below what a middle-class person would consider necessary for respectability. If they are "ambitious," they are likely to be ambitious for a working-class job recognized by their mates as better than the average job available or better than that from which they started. They do not typically aspire to middle-class jobs. Bakke even found that those who aspire for a foremanship are relatively few. They take satisfaction in a "swell job," but in evaluating a job as "swell" or otherwise they give little weight to its value as a stepping stone to a still better job, in sharp contrast to middle-class people, ever alert to prospects of "advancement" and "promotion."

"Planning" and "foresight" on the part of his parents are not so likely to be evident to the working-class as to the middle-class child. It is good to have something "laid by for a rainy day" but the pinch of the present is a more potent stimulus than the threat or promise of the future. A run of good luck is often more likely to result in an immediate rise in the level of living than in an exercise of asceticism and provision for the future. Provision for the future, in turn, is more likely to be concerned with maintaining an accustomed level of living than with raising it. Perhaps more remarkable than the contrast between the classes in spending patterns is the contrast in attitudes towards the acquisition of potentially remunerative skills. "Foresight" tends not to include an alertness to learning opportunities which might later "pay off." The job is evaluated in the light of its present yield in income, other immediate satisfactions and job security. It is not seen as a stage in an upward career.

A particularly significant contrast is that between what we have called the middle-class "ethic of individual responsibility" and the "ethic of reciprocity" to which the working-class, particularly its "lower-lower" and "underprivileged" levels, tends.[8] The "ethic of reciprocity" means a readiness to turn for aid to others toward whom one stands in a particularistic, primary-group relationship, a readiness to draw, with no feeling of guilt, upon their resources, and a corresponding sense of obligation to share one's own resources with them when they happen to be less fortunately situated. When carried to an extreme, such an ethic provides a sort of cushion of economic security, albeit of a very low level, and at the same time militates against "getting ahead" by the members of a group governed by such an ethic. It seems probable that not only economic reciprocity but ethical obligations in general, such as honesty, tend to be conceived more in particularistic terms in working-class society.

In general, the working-class person appears to be more dependent upon and "at home" in primary groups and to avoid secondary, segmental and formal relationships more than the middle-class person. He appears to be more spontaneous, emotionally irrepressible and "anarchic," to give freer and less disguised expression to his aggression, and to find it more difficult to play roles with which he does not basically identify. He is less likely to possess, to value or to cultivate the polish, the sophistication, the fluency, the "good appearance" and the "personality" so useful in "selling oneself" and manipulating others in the middle-class world.[9]

These are some of the ways in which the working-class boy is less likely than the middle-class boy to find the middle-class norms which we have described exemplified and taken for granted in the models provided by his family and neighborhood. To this extent he is less likely to identify with those norms, to "make them his own," and to be able to conform to them easily and "naturally."

SOCIAL CLASSES AS TRAINING GROUNDS

CHILDREN in different classes do not only differ with respect to the cultural models available in their milieux. The demands and expectations of others and the means of fulfilling them, the degree to which the child's environment and activities are deliberately structured by adults, the nature of rewards and punishments and the things for which they are administered are likely to be different.

Middle-class socialization, in comparison with working-class socialization, is conscious, rational, deliberate and demanding. Relatively little is left to chance and "just-growing." Middle-class parents are likely to be concerned and anxious about their children's achievement of age-graded "norms," and this anxiety is likely to be communicated to the child. They are more geared to a timetable, to the future as well as the present. The child is constantly aware of what his parents want him to *be* and to *become*. He learns early to take the long view and becomes habituated to the self-discipline and effort necessary to meeting parental expectations. His parents smile not only on achievement but on *effort*, even if unattended by success, and effort itself becomes a cardinal virtue.

Middle-class people are more likely deliberately to contrive the child's physical environment, his social milieu and the budgeting of his time with a view to hastening his socialization in the middle-class way of life. They surround him with books and with toys selected for their "educational" value. They supervise closely his friends and activities; to a marked degree they censor and manipulate them. They emphasize order, punctuality, time-consciousness—"a time and a place for everything." The middle-class child is more likely to eat and sleep by schedule, to retire at an early and regular hour, to be present at the family meal. His parents are more likely to expect him to segregate certain periods for home study, to attend Sunday school, and to take some kind of lessons or classes outside of regular school hours. They are more likely to define "a time for work and a time for play." They will cooperate more with the school, the church and other agencies outside the home to see that the child's time is not "wasted" and that he conforms to the expectations of these other middle-class figures as well.[10]

The middle-class child is probably more powerfully motivated to conform to parental expectations than is the working-class child. The middle-class home is likely to generate in the child a "need" for, a dependence upon parental love to an unusual degree. This love is not only a supreme value to the child. It is, in Margaret Mead's term, "conditional love." It is something to be merited, to be earned by effort and achievement. To the degree that this love is precarious and contingent, there is generated what Allison Davis calls an "adaptive" or "socialized" anxiety, which is to be allayed only by avoidance of proscribed behavior and by constant striving.

Working-class socialization, particularly in the lower-lower levels, tends to be relatively easy-going. The child's activities are more likely to be governed by his own present inclinations, his parents' convenience and momentary and unpremeditated impulses, and by the requirements of the household. They are less likely to be governed by exacting specifications of effort and achievement which are regarded as good in themselves or good because they are seen as instrumental to some long-range goals. Weaning and toilet training are likely to start later and the child is more likely to be picked up when he cries and to be fed when he is hungry. Later, with respect to eating, sleeping, cleanliness, dress, work, school and play he is allowed more latitude than the middle-class child. It has been suggested that because of this more "permissive" socialization the working-class child is likely to experience less frustration than the middle-class child. This does not necessarily follow and would certainly be difficult to demonstrate. The important thing is that the frustrations of the working-class child are not to the same degree the result of systematic pressure to master certain skills by a certain time or the cost, so to speak, of the achievement of deferred goals.

Again, it would be difficult to establish that the working-class child actually learns less or learns more slowly than the middle-class child. The important differences are in the nature of the skills and the values which are learned and in the motivation to learning. The working-class child is more often thrown upon his own or the company of an autonomous group of peers. He is freer to explore in many areas forbidden to the middle-class child and to encounter a variety of troubles, scrapes and personally meaningful problems. His learning is likely to be a product of "having fun" or to be motivated by the solution of immediate practical problems. Motivation to work for remote goals attainable only by rational, systematic, self-denying discipline is weak, because the discipline itself is not recognized as a virtue deserving of reward by his parents.

Furthermore, it is likely that the sanctions which the working-class parents administer are less effective than those of middle-class parents. It is doubtful that the effects of physical punishment, which is more common in the working-class, are as lasting or as deterrent as the effects of the threat of the loss of love. Because of the structure of the working-class home, the working-class child is less likely to develop the overwhelming emotional dependency on the love of one or two adults so typical of the middle-class child. The love itself, in turn, is not likely to be systematically contingent upon achievement as it is in the middle-class home.

At the same time, it seems likely, although this aspect of differential socialization has not been so well explored, that the working-class child is more dependent emotionally and for the satisfaction of many practical needs upon his relationships to his peer groups. He engages in more activities and spends more time in their company. Satisfactory emotional relationships with his peers are likely to be more important, their claims to be more imperious, and the rewards they offer to compete more effectively with parental expectations.

Physical prowess and aggression have also a different significance in middle-class and working-class socialization. In both classes physical competence and a readiness to stand and fight when attacked are important expectations of the male role. There are, however, important differences of emphasis. In the working-class, fighting is more likely to be recognized as a normal, natural and legitimate way of settling disputes. The working-class boy is more likely to see his parents and other adults fighting on what would seem to middle-class parents inadequate provocation to an

inherently degrading activity. His parents are likely to encourage physical combat where middle-class parents would
emphasize "reason" and diplomatic maneuver. And he may
even find his parents jumping into the fray rather than
pouring oil on troubled waters. In the middle class, fighting is a dubious way of settling issues. Physical prowess,
as a criterion of status, tends to be channelized into organized, competitive sports, governed by strict rules of "fair
play." In this way, it tends to become relegated to a special
context, the gym and the ball field, segregated from other
activities. It becomes another avenue of middle-class
achievement involving practice, training, self-discipline
and observance of rigid and impersonal rules.

RESULTANT PERSONALITY DIFFERENCES

THERE HAS been a lot of research on social class differences in socialization experiences. There is still a critical
shortage of research on the *outcome* of these differences,
on their consequences for the child's and the adolescent's
personality. That literature which does exist, however,
even if it is mostly impressionistic and lacking in statistical
precision, indicates that the results of this differential
socialization are just about what one might expect: that the
personalities of the children of the several classes are in
general younger versions of the personalities of their
parents.

On one phase of this matter there is no dearth of research. It may be taken as established that ability, as measured by performance in conventional tests of intelligence,

varies directly with social class.[11] Scores in such tests depend, of course, upon the kinds of skills which are considered important by those who construct and use the tests. In actual fact, the principal types of questions concern the understanding and handling of "bookish" language and skill in seeing geometrical and other mathematical relationships. It does not follow that one could not, conceivably, construct tests emphasizing other skills and in which working-class children would be equal or superior to middle-class children. Be that as it may, the conventional tests do test for abilities that are highly prized by middle-class people, that are fostered by middle-class socialization, and that are especially important for further achievement in the academic world and in middle-class society. In short, the results of these tests are one important index of the ability of the child to meet middle-class expectations, to do the kinds of things that bring rewards in the middle-class world.

On no other aspect of the consequences of differential socialization do we have such copious and definitive data. Significant research on differences in value systems and on behavior expressive of these values is not, however, altogether lacking.[12] Among the most important contributions in this area are Havighurst and Taba's *Adolescent Character and Personality** and Hollingshead's *Elmtown's Youth*.†

The general import of this research is that in manners and

---

*Robert J. Havighurst and Hilda Taba, *Adolescent Character and Personality* (New York: John Wiley and Sons, 1949).

†August B. Hollingshead, *Elmtown's Youth* (New York: John Wiley and Sons, 1949).

morals, in social as well as in intellectual skills, in work, in school and in play, the middle-class child is more likely to conform to the middle-class norms.

At the same time that we stress these social class differences in central tendency, it is important also to note the variability within classes, and especially within the working-class. Indeed, it seems probable that most children in American society, of whatever class, assimilate to some degree the middle-class value system. Some assimilate it in almost "pure" form, others in various attentuated versions and various uneasy combinations with the working-class value system, sometimes submerged by the working-class system but rarely altogether stifled.

Of special interest in this connection is William F. Whyte's* distinction between "corner boys" and "college boys," based upon his observations in an Italian slum in a large American city. Both types of boys are products of working-class families and neighborhoods, but they are radically different in their values and in the content and organization of their activities. The corner boy's life is organized around what we have called working-class values. The college boy is a working-class boy who has assumed middle-class values and behavior. One of the major themes of Whyte's book, *Street Corner Society*, is that the corner-boy way of life, although it yields satisfactions of its own, notably, those that derive from full and intimate participation in a close-knit primary group, militates against vertical mobility; the college-boy way of life, on the other

---

*William F. Whyte, *Street Corner Society* (Chicago: University of Chicago Press, 1937).

hand, fits into "a pattern of activity leading toward social mobility" and is, indeed, a prerequisite of such mobility. Clearly, then, there is no destiny which ordains that working-class boys will become embodiments of working-class values. For that matter, we cannot even assume that all working-class boys can be neatly classified as "corner boy" or "college boy." We need to know much more about the variability as well as the modal types of personalities in the different classes.

An example of one type of research which can further our knowledge of these matters is a study by Miss Leanna K. Barker of 75 "working-class" and 71 "middle-class" boys in an Indiana junior high school. A series of questions was designed to pose dilemmas which could be resolved by a solution embodying "working-class" (or "corner-boy") or "middle-class" (or "college-boy") values. Since the findings have not yet been published, some representative items and results will be presented here.[13]

Do you ever like to play or do things by yourself? It was assumed that working-class boys are more dependent upon the society of their peers, that middle-class boys are more likely to find satisfaction in independent activity. Seventy-six per cent of the middle-class boys, forty-three per cent of the working-class boys answered "yes" to this question.

Do you have any hobbies? For instance, do you collect or make things, do you play an instrument, or do you raise animals? It was assumed that the cultivation of hobbies reflects the middle-class emphasis on the "constructive" use of leisure, on the conception of time as a commodity that ought not to be "wasted" entirely in random and idle play.

Seventy-six per cent of the middle-class boys, thirty-seven per cent of the working-class boys answered "yes."

Suppose you and some of your friends go to a movie. One of the boys hasn't any money and you have some extra. O.K., you lend him the money. Now, in the bunch that you run with, what would you usually do? Would you expect him to (a) *pay you back or* (b) *just do you a favor sometime?* This question was designed to pit the middle-class conception of mutual aid as a quasi-contractual relationship, a sort of business transaction, against the working-class ethic of reciprocity ("You help me out when you're ahead of the game and I'll help you out when I'm ahead of the game"). Fifty-five per cent of the middle-class boys, seventy-six per cent of the working-class boys chose the second response.

A group of ten boys form a club. They all decide to go to Indianapolis to the auto races. It will cost about $6.00 a boy. They all get jobs and save their money for awhile. When the time of the races comes, they all have their money except one boy who is broke. One of his friends has earned and saved some extra money and says, "I'll pay your way." But the boy without money says, "No, you worked hard and saved the money. The money is yours and I have no right to it." The other boy says, "Yes, but you're my friend and friends are supposed to help one another. I'll pay your way. Even if you can't pay me back, that's O.K." Do you think the boy should let his friend pay his way, even if he's not sure he can pay it back? This question was designed to pose, in even sharper form, the same dilemma as the preceding question. Here the issue is raised of whether it is legitimate to accept aid from a primary group associate even if one is not sure he can repay it. The spirit of spontaneous giving and guiltless acceptance is pitted against the spirit of rational exchange and individual responsibility. Thirty-two per cent of the middle-class boys, sixty-three per cent of the working-class boys said "yes."

When these ten boys first thought of making this trip, nine of the boys were all excited about going and wanted to go very much. But one boy said, "It takes a long time to save $6.00. I'm studying to be an electrician and I'm saving to buy books and tools that will run me over $15.00. No, I can't afford to take this trip." All the other boys said: "The whole club ought to go together. Maybe it will take you a little longer to save your $15.00, but you won't feel right if you stay behind, and besides, the club ought to go as a whole." Do you think the boy should (a) *go along with the rest of the club or* (b) *stay home?* This question really involves two dilemmas: the long-run *versus* the short-run, and the corner boy emphasis on primary-group solidarity and loyalty *versus* the college-boy emphasis on personal advancement. Thirty-four per cent of the middle-class boys, fifty-one per cent of the working-class boys chose to "go along with the rest of the club."

Suppose you are out playing ball with the boys and having lots of fun. Do you (a) *leave the boys and go home to eat because you are expected home for meals at a certain time, or* (b) *go home to eat whenever you get hungry or through playing or whenever you feel like it?* The issue here is between middle-class time-consciousness, with its implications of punctuality, time-budgeting and self-dis-

cipline, and working-class preoccupation with the pleas-
ures and pains of the here and now. Eighty-seven per cent
of the middle-class boys, sixty-nine per cent of the working-
class boys give the first answer.

These and other of Miss Barker's data support the view
that the value systems which govern the conduct of middle-class and working-class boys do indeed emphasize
different aspirations, virtues and satisfactions. At the same
time, these data warn us against facile overgeneralization.
For every item cited, there were working-class boys who
gave "college-boy" responses and middle-class boys who
gave "corner-boy" responses. Furthermore, the distribution of responses is different for each item: the boy who
gives a "corner-boy" response to one item may give a "college-boy" response to another. As we suggested earlier,
there is no one-to-one correspondence between social class
and value systems. It is probable that nearly every American boy has internalized both corner-boy and college-boy
values and that even within a given social class the degree
to which the one or the other set of values is dominant
varies from individual to individual. Miss Barker's data
were secured by the administration of written questionnaires. The present writer, in an earlier and less carefully
controlled study, presented many of the same questions in
interview form and was impressed by the visible struggle
that most boys of any social level went through in answer-
ing such questions as those concerning the trip to Indianapolis. Although each boy is compelled, by the structure of
the questionnaire, to resolve each dilemma by a clear-cut
choice between the corner-boy and the college-boy alterna-

tive, and although working-class and middle-class boys may typically resolve these dilemmas in different ways, the resolution may represent the triumph, sometimes by a narrow margin, of one value system over a weaker but nonetheless serious competitor.

THE BOTTOM OF THE HEAP: PROBLEMS OF THE WORKING-CLASS BOY

THIS BOOK is an essay on the delinquent subculture, not on social class in America. To the reader it may seem that the path we have chosen to our destination is rather indirect. We have chosen this route not because we are enamored of indirection but because the shorter and easier routes have so often proved disappointing. Remember our problem: what is it about the structure of American society that produces, in certain sectors of that society, a subculture of a certain distinctive content? We do not believe that there is any simple answer to that question. We believe that it is necessary, in order to arrive at a satisfactory solution, to discover those combinations of personality and situation which yield the problems of adjustment to which the delinquent subculture is an appropriate response, and to show how these personalities and situations are generated by the life-conditions in those sectors in which that subculture prevails. There are many links in such an argument, and the weakness of any one may shake the plausibility of the whole. A spurious plausibility may sometimes be achieved by leaving certain vital assumptions unspoken and hence less likely to attract critical appraisal. The more explicit we make each link in the argument, the more we facilitate the task of the critic. Inviting criticism in this manner is not a masochistic gesture. None of us enjoys the public mutilation of the theories on which we have long labored and with which we have become identified. However, if there is anything of merit in those theories, it is out of such criticism that there grows the further research and the logical reconstruction of the arguments which are necessary to bring theories into closer correspondence with the reality they are designed to explain. If there are fundamental flaws in the argument some critic, friendly or otherwise, will eventually bring them to light anyway, and it is vouchsafed to very few to propound an explanation of a complex social phenomenon so logically neat and so empirically well grounded as to remain indefinitely invulnerable to criticism.

In the foregoing discussion of social class we have laid the groundwork for a better understanding of the problems of adjustment which we believe play a vital role in the genesis of the delinquent subculture. First and most obviously, the working class child shares the social class status of his parents. In the status game, then, the working-class child starts out with a handicap and, to the extent that he cares what middle-class persons think of him or has internalized the dominant middle-class attitudes toward social class position, he may be expected to feel some "shame." Margaret Mead has put the point with characteristi trenchancy if somewhat dubious melodrama:

Shame is felt perhaps most strongly over the failures of other people, especially one's parents, who have not been successful, who have not worked hard enough to have an inside bathroom or an automobile or to send one to a private school, to live on the right street, or go to the right church. As class is an expression of economic success, then it follows that to belong as a child or an adolescent in a class below others is a statement that one's parents have failed, they did not make good. This is bad enough when they have not risen, unbearable if they have started to fall even lower. Deeper than our disapproval of any breaking of the ten commandments lies our conviction that a failure to keep moving is an unforgiveable sin.*

Furthermore, people of status tend to be people of power and property. They have the means to make more certain that their children will obtain respect and other rewards which have status significance even where title in terms of deserving middle-class conduct is dubious. Hollingshead, in his *Elmtown's Youth,* stresses throughout the importance of parental status in obtaining special consideration in school activities and on the job through "connections" and other means of exerting pressure. Finally, parents of good standing in the class system can usually provide their children with money, clothes, cars, homes and other material amenities which not only function as external trappings and insignia of status, but which serve also as means and avenues to activities and relationships which confer status. Like his parents, a child is unlikely to be invited to participate in activities which require a material apparatus he cannot afford; if invited, he is less likely to accept for fear of embarrassment; and if he accepts, he is less likely to be in a position to reciprocate and therefore to sustain a relationship premised on a certain amount of

---

*Margaret Mead, *op. cit.,* p. 197.

reciprocity. It seems reasonable to assume that out of all this there arise feelings of inferiority and perhaps resentment and hostility. It is remarkable, however, that there is relatively little research explicitly designed to test this assumption.

However, invidious status distinctions among young people are, after all, a result of individual differences in conformity to a set of conduct norms as well as simple functions of their parents' social status. Havighurst and Taba in their *Adolescent Character and Personality* have shown that variations in "character reputation" scores cannot be explained simply as a result of social class membership. The existence of "achieved" as well as "ascribed" criteria of status for children makes it possible for some working-class children to "rise above" the status to which the social class position of their parents would otherwise consign them. However, this does not make the situation psychologically any easier for those of their brethren who remain behind, or rather, below. Low achieved status is no pleasanter than low ascribed status, and very likely a good deal more unpleasant, for reasons we have indicated earlier; it reflects more directly on the *personal* inadequacy of the child and leaves him with fewer convenient rationalizations.

One of the situations in which children of all social levels come together and compete for status in terms of the same set of middle-class criteria and in which working-class children are most likely to be found wanting is in the school. American educators are enamored of the idea of "democracy" as a goal of the schools. An examination of their writings reveals that "democracy" signifies "the fullest realization of the individual's potentialities," "the development of skills to an optimal level," "the development of character and abilities which can be admired by others," "preparation for effective participation in the adult vocational world."[14] Despite reservations such as "with due regard to individual differences," this conception of "democratic" education implies that a major function of the schools is to "promote," "encourage," "motivate," "stimulate," in brief, *reward* middle-class ambition and conformity to middle-class expectations. However sincerely one may desire to avoid odious comparisons and to avoid, thereby, injury to the self-esteem of those who do not conform to one's expectations, it is extremely difficult to reward, however subtly, successful conformity without at the same time, by implication, condemning and punishing the non-conformist. That same teacher who prides himself on his recognition and encouragement of deserving working-class children dramatizes, by that very show of pride, the superior merit of the "college-boy" working-class child to his less gifted or "corner-boy" working-class classmates.[15]

There are three good reasons why status in the school, insofar as it depends upon recognition by the teacher, should be measured by middle-class standards.

First, the teacher is *hired* to foster the development of middle-class personalities. The middle-class board of education, the middle-class parents whom they represent and, it is to be presumed, many of the working-class parents as well expect the teacher to define his job as the indoctrination of middle-class aspirations, character, skills and manners.[16]

Second, the teacher himself is almost certain to be a middle-class person, who personally values ambition and achievement and spontaneously recognizes and rewards these virtues in others.[17]

The third relates to the school itself as a social system with certain "structural imperatives" of its own. The teacher's textbooks in education and his own supervisors may stress "individualization" and "consideration for the needs, limitations and special problems of each student." Nonetheless, the teacher actually handles 20, 30 or 40 students at a time. Regardless of what he conceives his proper function to be, he necessarily looks with favor on the quiet, cooperative, "well-behaved" pupils who make his job easier and with disapproval and vexation on the lusty, irrepressible, boisterous youngsters who are destructive of order, routine and predictability in the classroom. Furthermore, the teacher himself is likely to be upwardly mobile or at least anxious about the security of his tenure in his present job. He is motivated, therefore, to conform to the criteria in terms of which *his* superiors evaluate *him*. Those superiors may themselves be "progressive" and in teacher meetings preach "democracy in the classroom" and "individualization" and indeed genuinely believe in those goals. However, the degree to which a teacher tries to achieve these goals or succeeds in doing so is not highly visible and readily determined. On the other hand, grades, performance on standardized examinations, the cleanliness and orderliness of the classroom and the frequency with which children are sent to the "front office" are among the most easily determined and "objective" bases for the evaluation of teacher performance. A good "rating," then, by his supervisors is possible only if the teacher sacrifices to some degree the very "individualization" and "toler-ance" which those same supervisors may urge upon him.

Research on the kinds of behavior which teachers regard as the most "problematical" among their pupils gives results consistent with our expectations. [18] The most serious problems, from the standpoint of the teacher, are those children who are restless and unruly, who fidget and squirm, who annoy and distract, who create "discipline" problems. The "good" children are the studious, the obedi-ent, the docile. It is precisely the working-class children who are most likely to be "problems" because of their rela-tive lack of training in order and discipline, their lack of interest in intellectual achievement and their lack of rein-forcement by the home in conformity to the requirements of the school. Both in terms of "conduct" and in terms of academic achievement, the failures in the classroom are drawn disproportionately from the lower social class levels. The child has little or no choice in selecting the group within which he shall compete for status and, in the words of Troyer, he is "evaluated against the total range of the ability distribution."

It is here that, day after day, most of the children in the lower fourth of the distribution have their sense of worth des-troyed, develop feelings of insecurity, become frustrated and lose confidence in their ability to learn even that which they are capable of learning.*

In settlement houses and other adult-sponsored and managed recreational agencies similar conflicts may often be seen between the middle-class values of the adults in charge and the working-class values of the children for whose benefit the institutions ostensibly exist. Such organizations smile upon neat, orderly, polite, personable, mannerly children who "want to make something of themselves." The sponsors, directors and group work leaders find it a pleasure to work with such children, whose values are so like their own, and make them feel welcome and respected. They do indeed feel a special responsibility toward the boy whose family and neighborhood culture have not equipped him with those values, the "rough" boy, the "dirty" boy, the "bum" who just "hangs around" with the gang on the corner, in the pool hall or in the candy store. But the responsibility they feel toward him is to encourage him to engage in more "worthwhile" activities, to join and to be a "responsible" member of some "wholesome" adult-supervised club or other group, to expurgate his language and, in general, to participate in the "constructive" program of the institution. Indeed, like the school, it functions to select potentially upwardly mobile working-class children and to help and encourage them in the upward climb. It is a common experience of such organizations that they "are very successful and do a lot

---

*Maurice E. Troyer, "Squaring Evaluation Processes with Democratic Values," *American Council of Education Studies*, Series I, No. 34 (January, 1949), 42.

of good but don't seem to get the children who need them most." The reason is that here, as in the school, it is almost impossible to reward one kind of behavior without at the same time, by implication or quite openly, punishing its absence or its opposite. The corner boy, as Whyte[19] has shown vividly and in detail, quickly senses that he is under the critical or at best condescending surveillance of people who are "foreigners" to his community and who appraise him in terms of values which he does not share. He is aware that he is being invidiously compared to others; he is uncomfortable; he finds it hard to accommodate himself to the rules of the organization. To win the favor of the people in charge he must change his habits, his values, his ambitions, his speech and his associates. Even were these things possible, the game might not be worth the candle. So, having sampled what they have to offer, he returns to the street or to his "clubhouse" in a cellar where "facilities"are meager but human relations more satisfying.

Not only in terms of standards of middle-class adults but in terms of their children's standards as well, the working-class boy of working-class culture is likely to be a "failure." Despite the existence among middle-class children of a "youth culture" which may differ in significant ways from the culture of their parents, the standards these children apply are likely to relegate to an inferior status their working-class peers. Coyle quotes from a fieldworker's report:

Gradually the group became more critical of prospective members. A process somewhat evident from the beginning became more obvious. In general only boys who measured up to the group's unwritten, unspoken and largely unconscious standards were ever considered. These standards, characteristics of their middle-class homes, required the suppression of impulsive disorderly behavior and put a high value on controlled cooperative attitudes. Hence even these normally healthy and boisterous boys were capable of rejecting schoolmates they considered too wild and boisterous. Coincident with this was an emphasis on intellectual capacity and achievement. They preferred "smart" as contrasted with "dumb" prospects. The boys seemed to use their club unconsciously to express and reinforce the standards learned in their homes and the community.*

Havighurst and Taba point out that not only teachers but schoolmates, in evaluating the character of other children, tend to give the highest ratings to the children of the higher social levels, although the correlation between social class and character reputation is far from perfect.† Positive correlations between various indices of social class status of the home and social status in the school as measured by pupils' choices have been found by Bonney and others.‡ Hollingshead has shown how social class and the behavior and personality associated with social class membership operate to determine prestige and clique and date patterns among high school boys and girls. "This process operates in all classes, but it is especially noticeable in contacts with class V [lower-lower]. This class is so repug-

---

*Grace L. Coyle, *Group Work with American Youth, A Guide to the Practice of Leadership* (New York: Harper and Brothers, 1948), p. 49.

†Robert J. Havighurst and Hilda Taba, *op. cit.,* pp. 52-55.

‡Merl E. Bonney, "A Study of Social Status on the Second Grade Level," *Journal of Genetic Psychology.* LX (June, 1942), 271-305. See also Henry P. Smith, "A Study in the Selective Character of American Secondary Education: Participation in School Activities as Conditioned by Socio-Economic Status and Other Factors," *Journal of Educational Psychology,* XXXVI (April, 1945), 229-246 and August B. Hollingshead, *op. cit.,* pp. 192-203.

nant socially that adolescents in the higher classes avoid clique and dating ties with its members."* Furthermore, working-class children are less likely to participate, and if they participate are less likely to achieve prominence, in extra-curricular activities, which are an important arena for the competition for status in the eyes of the students themselves. In the area of organized athletics the working-class boy is perhaps least unfitted for successful competition. Even here, however, he is likely to be at a disadvantage. Adherence to a training regimen and a schedule does not come to him as easily as to the middle-class boy and, unless he chooses to loosen his ties to his working-class friends, he is likely to find some conflict between the claims of the gang and those of his athletic career. Finally, although we must not minimize the importance of athletic achievement as a status-ladder, it is, after all, granted to relatively few, of whatever social class background, to achieve conspicuously in this area.[20]

In summary, it may confidently be said that the working-class boy, particularly if his training and values be those we have here defined as working-class, is more likely than his middle-class piers to find himself at the bottom of the status hierarchy whenever he moves in a middle-class world, whether it be of adults or of children. To the degree to which he values middle-class status, either because he values the good opinion of middle-class persons or because he has to some degree internalized middle-class standards himself, he faces a problem of adjustment and is in the market for a "solution."

---

*August B. Hollingshead, *op cit.*, p. 241.

CHAPTER V

A Delinquent Solution

WHAT THE DELINQUENT SUBCULTURE HAS TO OFFER

THE DELINQUENT subculture, we suggest, is a way of dealing with the problems of adjustment we have described. These problems are chiefly status problems: certain children are denied status in the respectable society because they cannot meet the criteria of the respectable status system. The delinquent subculture deals with these problems by providing criteria of status which these children *can* meet.

This statement is highly elliptical and is based upon a number of assumptions whose truth is by no means self-evident. It is not, for example, self-evident that people whose status positions are low must necessarily feel deprived, injured or ego-involved in that low status. Whether they will or not depends upon several considerations.

We remarked earlier that our ego-involvement in a given comparison with others depends upon our "status universe." "Whom do we measure ourselves against?" is the crucial question. In some other societies virtue may consist in willing acceptance of the role of peasant, low-born commoner or member of an inferior caste and in conformity to the expectations of that role. If others are richer, more nobly-born or more able than oneself, it is by the will of an inscrutable Providence and not to be imputed to one's own moral defect. The sting of status inferiority is thereby removed or mitigated; one measures himself only against those of like social position. We have suggested, however, that an important feature of American "democracy," perhaps of the Western European tradition in general, is the tendency to measure oneself against "all comers." This means that, for children as for adults, one's sense of personal worth is at stake in status comparisons with all other persons, at least of one's own age and sex, whatever their family background or material circumstances. It means that, in the lower levels of our status hierarchies, whether adult or juvenile, there is a chronic fund of motivation, conscious or repressed, to elevate one's status position, either by striving to climb within the established status system or by redefining the criteria of status so that one's present attributes become status-giving assets. It has been suggested, for example, that such typically working-class forms of Protestantism as the Holiness sects owe their appeal to the fact that they reverse the respectable status system; it is the humble, the simple and the dispossessed who sit at the right hand of God, whereas worldly goods, power and knowledge are as nothing in His eyes. In like manner, we offer the view that the delinquent subculture is one solution to a kindred problem on the juvenile level.

Another consideration affecting the degree of privation experienced in a given status position is the "status source." A person's status, after all, is how he stands in somebody's eyes. Status, then, is not a fixed property of the person but varies with the point of view of whoever is doing the judging. I may be revered by some and despised by others. A crucial question then becomes: "Whose respect or admiration do I value?" That *you* think well or ill of me may or may not *matter* to me.

It may be argued that the working-class boy does not *care* what middle-class people think of him, that he is ego-involved only in the opinions of his family, his friends, his working-class neighbors. A definitive answer to this argument can come only from research designed to get at the facts. This research, in our opinion, is yet to be done. There is, however, reason to believe that most children are sensitive *to some degree* about the attitudes of *any persons* with whom they are thrown into more than the most superficial kind of contact. The contempt or indifference of others, particularly of those like schoolmates and teachers, with whom we are constrained to associate for long hours every day, is difficult, we suggest, to shrug off. It poses a problem with which one may conceivably attempt to cope in a variety of ways. One may make an active effort to change himself in conformity with the expectations of others; one may attempt to justify or explain away his inferiority in terms which will exculpate him; one may tell oneself that he really doesn't care what these people think; one may react with anger and aggression. But the least probable response is simple, uncomplicated, honest indifference. If we grant the probable truth of the claim that most American working-class children are most sensitive to status sources on their own level, it does not follow that they take lightly rejection, disparagement and censure from other status sources.

Even on their "own" social level, the situation is far from simple. The "working class," we have repeatedly emphasized, is not culturally homogeneous. Not only is there much diversity in the cultural standards applied by one's own working-class neighbors and kin so that it is difficult to find a "working-class" milieu in which "middle-class" standards are not important. In addition, the "working-class" culture we have described is, after all, an ideal type; most working-class *people* are culturally ambivalent. Due to lack of capacity, of the requisite "character structure" or of "luck," they may be working-class in terms of job and income; they may have accepted this status with resignation and rationalized it to their satisfaction; and by example, by class-linked techniques of child training and by failure to support the middle-class agencies of socialization they may have produced children deficient in the attributes that make for status in middle-class terms. Nevertheless, all their lives, through all the major media of mass indoctrination—the schools, the movies, the radio, the newspapers and the magazines—the middle-class powers-that-be that manipulate these media have been trying to "sell" them on middle-class values and the middle-class standard of living. Then there is the "propaganda of the deed," the fact that they have seen with their own eyes working-class contemporaries "get ahead" and "make the grade" in a middle-class world. In consequence of all this, we suspect that few working-class parents unequivocally repudiate as intrinsically worthless middle-class objectives. There is good reason to believe that the modesty of working-class aspirations is partly a matter of trimming one's sails to the available opportunities and resources and partly a matter of unwillingness to accept the discipline which upward striving entails.

However complete and successful one's accommodation to an humble status, the vitality of middle-class goals, of the "American dream," is nonetheless likely to manifest itself in his aspirations for his children. His expectations may not be grandiose, but he will want his children to be "better off" than he. Whatever his own work history and social reputation may be, he will want his children to be "steady" and "respectable." He may exert few positive pressures to "succeed" and the experiences he provides his children may even incapacitate them for success; he may be puzzled at the way they "turn out." But whatever the measure of his own responsibility in accounting for the product, he is not likely to judge that product by unadulterated "corner-boy" standards. Even "corner-boy" parents, although they may value in their children such corner-boy virtues as generosity to friends, personal loyalty and physical prowess, are likely also to be gratified by recognition by middle-class representatives and by the kinds of achievement for which the college-boy way of life is a prerequisite. Even in the working-class milieu from which he acquired his incapacity for middle-class achievement, the working-class corner-boy may find himself at a status disadvantage as against his more upwardly mobile peers.

Lastly, of course, is that most ubiquitous and inescapable of status sources, oneself. Technically, we do not call the person's attitudes towards himself "status" but rather "self-esteem," or, when the quality of the self-attitude is specifically moral, "conscience" or "superego." The important question for us is this: To what extent, if at all, do boys who are typically "working-class" and "corner-boy" in their overt behavior evaluate themselves by "middle-class," "college-boy" standards? For our overt behavior, however closely it conforms to one set of norms, need not argue against the existence or effectiveness of alternative and conflicting norms. The failure of our own behavior to conform to our own expectations is an elementary and commonplace fact which gives rise to the tremendously important consequences of guilt, self-recrimination, anxiety and self-hatred. The reasons for the failure of self-expectations and overt conduct to agree are complex. One reason is that we often internalize more than one set of norms, each of which would dictate a different course of action in a given life-situation; since we can only *do* one thing at a time, however, we are forced to choose between them or somehow to compromise. In either case, we fall short of the full realization of our own expectations and must somehow cope with the residual discrepancy between those expectations and our overt behavior.

We have suggested that corner-boy children (like their working-class parents) internalize middle-class standards to a sufficient degree to create a fundamental ambivalence towards their own corner-boy behavior. Again, we are on somewhat speculative ground where fundamental research remains to be done. The coexistence within the same personality of a corner-boy and a college-boy morality may appear more plausible, however, if we recognize that they are not simple antitheses of one another and that parents and others may in all sincerity attempt to indoctrinate both. For example, the goals upon which the college-boy places such great value, such as intellectual and occupational achievement, and the college-boy virtues of ambitiousness and pride in self-sufficiency are not as such disparaged by the corner-boy culture. The meritoriousness of standing by one's friends and the desire to have a good time here and now do not by definition preclude the desire to help oneself and to provide for the future. It is no doubt the rule, rather than the exception, that most children, college-boy and corner-boy alike, would like to enjoy the best of both worlds. *In practice*, however, the substance that is consumed in the pursuit of one set of values is not available for the pursuit of the other. The sharpness of the dilemma and the degree of the residual discontent depend upon a number of things, notably, the intensity with which both sets of norms have been internalized, the extent to which the life-situations which one encounters compel a choice between them, and the abundance and appropriateness of the skills and resources at one's disposal. The child of superior intelligence, for example, may find it easier than his less gifted peers to meet the demands of the college-boy standards without failing his obligations to his corner-boy associates.

It is a plausible assumption, then, that the working-class boy whose status is low in middle-class terms *cares* about that status, that this status confronts him with a genuine problem of adjustment. To this problem of adjustment there are a variety of conceivable responses, of which participation in the creation and the maintenance of the delinquent subculture is one. Each mode of response entails costs and yields gratifications of its own. The circumstances which tip the balance in favor of the one or the other are obscure. One mode of response is to desert the corner-boy for the college-boy way of life. To the reader of Whyte's *Street Corner Society* the costs are manifest. It is hard, at best, to be a college-boy and to run with the corner-boys. It entails great effort and sacrifice to the degree that one has been indoctrinated in what we have described as the working-class socialization process; its rewards are frequently long-deferred; and for many working-class boys it makes demands which they are, in consequence of their inferior linguistic, academic and "social" skills, not likely ever to meet. Nevertheless, a certain proportion of working-class boys accept the challenge of the middle-class status system and play the status game by the middle-class rules.

Another response, perhaps the most common, is what we may call the "stable corner-boy response." It represents an acceptance of the corner-boy way of life and an effort to make the best of a situation. If our reasoning is correct, it does not resolve the dilemmas we have described as inherent in the corner-boy position in a largely middle-class world, although these dilemmas may be mitigated by an effort to disengage oneself from dependence upon middle-class status-sources and by withdrawing, as far as possible, into a sheltering community of like-minded working-class children. Unlike the delinquent response, it avoids the radical rupture of good relations with even working-class adults and does not represent as irretrievable a renunciation of upward mobility. It does not incur the active hostility of middle-class persons and therefore leaves the way open to the pursuit of some values, such as jobs, which these people control. It represents a preference for the familiar, with its known satisfactions and its known imperfections, over the risks and the uncertainties as well as the moral costs of the college-boy response, on the one hand, and the delinquent response on the other.

What does the delinquent response have to offer? Let us be clear, first, about what this response is and how it differs from the stable corner-boy response. The hallmark of the delinquent subculture is the explicit and wholesale repudiation of middle-class standards and the adoption of their very antithesis. *The corner-boy culture is not specifically delinquent.* Where it leads to behavior which may be defined as delinquent, *e.g.,* truancy, it does so not because nonconformity to middle-class norms *defines* conformity to corner-boy norms but because conformity to middle-class norms *interferes with* conformity to corner-boy norms. The corner-boy plays truant because he does not like school, because he wishes to escape from a dull and unrewarding and perhaps humiliating situation. But truancy is not defined as intrinsically valuable and status-giving. The member of the delinquent subculture plays truant because "good" middle-class (and working-class) children do not play truant. Corner-boy resistance to being herded and marshalled by middle-class figures is not the same as the delinquent's flouting and jeering of those middle-class figures and active ridicule of those who submit. The corner-boy's ethic of reciprocity, his quasi-communal attitude toward the property of in-group members, is shared by the delinquent. But this ethic of reciprocity does not sanction the deliberate and "malicious" violation of the property rights of persons outside the in-group. We have observed that the differences between the corner-boy and the college-boy or middle-class culture are profound but that in many ways they are profound differences in emphasis. We have remarked that the corner-boy culture does not so much repudiate the value of many middle-class achievements as it emphasizes certain other values which make such achievements improbable. In short, the corner-boy culture temporizes with middle-class morality; the full-fledged delinquent subculture does not.

It is precisely here, we suggest, in the refusal to temporize, that the appeal of the delinquent subculture lies. Let us recall that it is characteristically American, not specifically working-class or middle-class, to measure oneself against the widest possible status universe, to seek status against "all comers," to be "as good as" or "better than" anybody—anybody, that is, within one's own age and sex category. As long as the working-class corner-boy clings to a version, however attenuated and adulterated, of the middle-class culture, he must recognize his inferiority to working-class and middle-class college-boys. The delinquent subculture, on the other hand, permits no ambiguity of the status of the delinquent relative to that of anybody else. In terms of the norms of the delinquent subculture, defined by its negative polarity to the respectable status system, the delinquent's very nonconformity to middle-class standards sets him above the most exemplary college boy.

Another important function of the delinquent subculture is the legitimation of aggression. We surmise that a certain amount of hostility is generated among working-class children against middle-class persons, with their airs of superiority, disdain or condescension and against middle-class norms, which are, in a sense, the cause of their status-frustration. To infer inclinations to aggression from the existence of frustration is hazardous; we know that aggression is not an inevitable and not the only consequence of frustration. So here too we must feel our way with caution. Ideally, we should like to see systematic research, probably employing "depth interview" and "projective" techniques, to get at the relationship between status position and aggressive dispositions toward the rules which determine status and toward persons variously distributed in the status hierarchy. Nevertheless, despite our imperfect knowledge of these things, we would be blind if we failed to recognize that bitterness, hostility and jealousy and all sorts of retributive fantasies are among the most common and typically human responses to public humiliation. However, for the child who temporizes with middle-class morality, overt aggression and even the conscious recognition of his own hostile impulses are inhibited, for he acknowledges the *legitimacy* of the rules in terms of which he is stigmatized. For the child who breaks clean with middle-class morality, on the other hand, there are no moral inhibitions on the free expression of aggression against the sources of his frustration. Moreover, the connection we suggest between status-frustration and the aggressiveness of the delinquent subculture seems to us more plausible than many frustration-aggression hypotheses because it involves no assumptions about obscure and dubious "displacement" of aggression against "substitute" targets. The target in this case is the manifest cause of the status problem.

It seems to us that the mechanism of "reaction-formation" should also play a part here. We have made much of the corner-boy's basic ambivalence, his uneasy acknowledgement, while he lives by the standards of his corner-boy culture, of the legitimacy of college-boy standards. May we assume that when the delinquent seeks to obtain unequivocal status by repudiating, once and for all, the norms of the college-boy culture, these norms really undergo total extinction? Or do they, perhaps, linger on, underground, as it were, repressed, unacknowledged but an ever-present threat to the adjustment which has been achieved at no small cost? There is much evidence from clinical psychology that moral norms, once effectively internalized, are not lightly thrust aside or extinguished. If a new moral order is evolved which offers a more satisfactory solution to one's life problems, the old order usually continues to press for recognition, but if this recognition is granted, the applecart is upset. The symptom of this obscurely felt, ever-present threat is clinically known as "anxiety," and the literature of psychiatry is rich with devices for combatting this anxiety, this threat to a hard-won victory. One such device is reaction-formation. Its hallmark is an "exaggerated," "disproportionate," "abnormal" intensity of response, "inappropriate" to the stimulus which seems to elicit it. The unintelligibility of the response, the "over-reaction," becomes intelligible when we see that it has the function of reassuring the actor against an *inner* threat to his defenses as well as the function of meeting an external situation on its own terms. Thus we have the mother who "compulsively" showers "inordinate" affection upon a child to reassure herself against her latent hostility and we have the male adolescent whose awkward and immoderate masculinity reflects a basic insecurity about his own sex-role. In like manner, we would expect the delinquent boy who, after all, has been socialized in a society dominated by a middle-class morality and who can never quite escape the blandishments of middle-class society, to seek to maintain his safeguards against seduction. Reaction-formation, in his case, should take the form of an "irrational," "malicious," "unaccountable" hostility to the enemy within the gates as well as without: the norms of the respectable middle-class society.[1]

If our reasoning is correct, it should throw some light upon the peculiar quality of "property delinquency" in the delinquent subculture. We have already seen how the rewardingness of a college-boy and middle-class way of life depends, to a great extent, upon general respect for property rights. In an urban society, in particular, the possession and display of property are the most ready and public badges of reputable social class status and are, for that reason, extraordinarily ego-involved. That property actually is a reward for middle-class morality is in part only a plausible fiction, but in general there is certainly a relationship between the practice of that morality and the possession of property. The middle-classes have, then, a strong interest in scrupulous regard for property rights, not only because property is "intrinsically" valuable but because the full enjoyment of their status requires that that status be readily recognizable and therefore that property adhere to those who earn it. The cavalier misappropriation or destruction of property, therefore, is not only a diversion or diminution of wealth; it is an attack on the middle-class where their egos are most vulnerable. Group stealing, institutionalized in the delinquent subculture, is not just a way of *getting* something. It is a means that is the antithesis of sober and diligent "labour in a calling." It expresses contempt for a way of life by making its opposite a criterion of status. Money and other valuables are not, as such, despised by the delinquent. For the delinquent and the non-delinquent alike, money is a most glamorous and efficient means to a variety of ends and one cannot have too much of it. But, in the delinquent subculture, the stolen dollar has an odor of sanctity that does not attach to the dollar saved or the dollar earned.

This delinquent system of values and way of life does

its job of problem-solving most effectively when it is adopted as a group solution. We have stressed in our chapter on the general theory of subcultures that the efficacy of a given change in values as a solution and therefore the motivation to such a change depends heavily upon the availability of "reference groups" within which the "deviant values" are already institutionalized, or whose members would stand to profit from such a system of deviant values if each were assured of the support and concurrence of the others. So it is with delinquency. We do not suggest that joining in the creation or perpetuation of a delinquent subculture is the only road to delinquency. We do believe, however, that for most delinquents delinquency would not be available as a response were it not socially legitimized and given a kind of respectability, albeit by a restricted community of fellow-adventurers. In this respect, the adoption of delinquency is like the adoption of the practice of appearing at the office in open-collar and shirt sleeves. Is it much more comfortable, is it more sensible than the full regalia? Is it neat? Is it dignified? The arguments in the affirmative will appear much more forceful if the practice is already established in one's milieu or if one senses that others are prepared to go along if someone makes the first tentative gestures. Indeed, to many of those who sweat and chafe in ties and jackets, the possibility of an alternative may not even occur until they discover that it has been adopted by their colleagues.

This way of looking at delinquency suggests an answer to a certain paradox. Countless mothers have protested that their "Johnny" was a good boy until he fell in with a certain bunch. But the mothers of each of Johnny's companions hold the same view with respect to their own offspring. It is conceivable and even probable that some of these mothers are naive, that one or more of these youngsters are "rotten apples" who infected the others. We suggest, however, that all of the mothers may be right, that there is a certain chemistry in the group situation itself which engenders that which was not there before, that group interaction is a sort of catalyst which releases potentialities not otherwise visible. This is especially true when we are dealing with a problem of status-frustration. Status, by definition, is a grant of respect from others. A new system of norms, which measures status by criteria which one can meet, is of no value unless others are prepared to apply those criteria, and others are not likely to do so unless one is prepared to reciprocate.[2]

We have referred to a lingering ambivalence in the delinquent's own value system, an ambivalence which threatens the adjustment he has achieved and which is met through the mechanism of reaction-formation. The delinquent may have to contend with another ambivalence, in the area of his status sources. The delinquent subculture offers him status *as against* other children of whatever social level, but it offers him this status *in the eyes of* his fellow delinquents only. To the extent that there remains a desire for recognition from groups whose respect has been forfeited by commitment to a new subculture, his satisfaction in his solution is imperfect and adulterated. He can perfect his solution only by rejecting as status sources those who reject him. This too may require a certain measure of reaction-formation, going beyond indifference to active hostility and contempt for all those who do not share his subculture. He becomes all the more dependent upon his delinquent gang. Outside that gang his status position is now weaker than ever. The gang itself tends toward a kind of sectarian solidarity, because the benefits of membership can only be realized in active face-to-face relationships with group members.

This interpretation of the delinquent subculture has important implications for the "sociology of social problems." People are prone to assume that those things which we define as evil and those which we define as good have their origins in separate and distinct features of our society. Evil flows from poisoned wells; good flows from pure and crystal fountains. The same source cannot feed both. Our view is different. It holds that those values which are at the core of "the American way of life," which help to motivate the behavior which we most esteem as "typically American," are among the major determinants of that which we stigmatize as "pathological." More specifically, it holds that the problems of adjustment to which the delinquent subculture is a response are determined, in part, by those very values which respectable society holds most sacred. The same value system, impinging upon children differently equipped to meet it, is instrumental in generating both delinquency and respectability.

WHAT ABOUT THE SEX DIFFERENCES?

MY SKIN has nothing of the quality of down or silk, there is nothing limpid or flute-like about my voice, I am a total loss with needle and thread, my posture and carriage are wholly lacking in grace. These imperfections cause me no distress—if anything, they are gratifying—because I conceive myself to be a man and want people to recognize me as a full-fledged, unequivocal representative of my sex. My wife, on the other hand, is not greatly embarrassed by her inability to tinker with or talk about the internal organs of a car, by her modest attainments in arithmetic or by her inability to lift heavy objects. Indeed, I am reliably informed that many women—I do not suggest that my wife is among them—often affect ignorance, frailty and emotional instability because to do otherwise would be out of keeping with a reputation for indubitable femininity.

In short, people do not simply want to excel; they want to excel *as a man* or *as a woman*, that is to say, in those respects which, in their culture, are symbolic of their respective sex roles. Furthermore, in seeking solutions to their problems of adjustment, they seek solutions that will not endanger their identification as essentially male or female. Even when they adopt behavior which is considered disreputable by conventional standards, the tendency is to be disreputable in ways that are characteristically masculine and feminine.

By the same token, I am not embarrassed or jealous because a colleague twenty years my senior has attained a loftier occupational position than I. In general, I am ego-involved only with respect to those attributes which are expectations and symbols of the distinctive roles, especially the age and sex categories, with which I identify. It is for this reason that, when we wrote that Americans measure themselves against "all comers," we added "of their own age and sex."

It follows from all this that the problems of adjustment of men and women, of boys and girls, arise out of quite different circumstances and press for quite different solutions. It is time now to consider some of the differences between the male and female roles which make the delinquent subculture which we have described peculiarly appropriate to the problems of the male child.

The reader will sense, although he may find it hard to articulate, that in some way both the respectable middle-class pattern and the delinquent response are characteristically *masculine*. Although they differ dramatically, to be sure, they have something in common. This common element is suggested by the words "achievement," "exploit," "aggressiveness," "daring," "active mastery," "pursuit." Every one of these terms has, to be sure, a different twist of emphasis or direction when combined with the different value orientations of the respectable and the delinquent cultures. For one thing, the *kinds* of achievement or exploit which are valued differ. For another, they are harnessed, disciplined, systematized and put in the service of long-run goals in the middle-class culture; in the delinquent subculture, they are affiliated with and transformed by impulsivity, short-run hedonism, violence and predation. In both cultures, however, one measures his manhood by comparing his *performance*, whether it be in stealing, fighting, athletic contests, work, or intellectual achievement, against that of others of his own sex. The delinquent response, however it may be condemned by others on moral grounds, has at least one virtue: it incontestably confirms, in the eyes of all concerned, his essential masculinity.

The delinquent is the rogue male. His conduct may be viewed not only negatively, as a device for attacking and derogating the respectable culture; positively it may be viewed as the exploitation of modes of behavior which are traditionally symbolic of untrammeled masculinity, which are renounced by middle-class culture because incompatible with its ends, but which are not without a certain aura of glamor and romance. For that matter, they find their way into the respectable culture as well but only in disciplined and attenuated forms as in organized sports, in fantasy and in make-believe games, or vicariously as in movies, television, and comic books. They are not, however, allowed to interfere with the serious business of life. The delinquent, on the other hand, having renounced this serious business, as defined by the middle class, is freer to divert these subterranean currents of our cultural tradition to his own use. The important point for our purpose is that the delinquent response, "wrong" though it may be and "disreputable," is well within the range of responses that do not threaten his identification of himself as a male.

Whereas the most highly ego-involved "region" of the boy's "life-space," to use the terminology of Kurt Lewin and his school, is that of performance and achievement relative to that of other boys, the corresponding highly ego-involved region for the girl is that of her relationships with the opposite sex. We do not suggest that girls are in any sense "naturally" more interested in boys than boys are in girls. We mean that the female's station in society, the admiration, respect and property that she commands, depend to a much greater degree on the kinds of relationships she establishes with members of the opposite sex.

This is perhaps more dramatically clear in adulthood. Social class status, we observed, is a status position shared by the members of a family; that, in turn, is determined primarily by the lineage, wealth, personal qualities and, above all, the occupational achievement of the husband and father. The claim to status based on characteristics of the male "head" must, of course, be validated by conformity of the rest of the family to certain proprieties. The wife and children, by improper behavior, can seriously "reflect on the family" and thus deprive it of some of the status to which it might otherwise be entitled. Nonetheless, the conduct of the other members of the family can do relatively little to *raise* the family's social position beyond the limits set by the prestige of the male parent. Furthermore, it is the male who carries the largest share of the *moral responsibility* for his family's status. His wife and children may feel shame if the family's position falls because of the father's unemployment, business failure, or other occupational or financial reverses, but the "fault" is likely to be imputed to the father and the burden of guilt to rest most heavily on him. It follows that the man's success in the adult role is, as compared with the woman's, less dependent upon whom he marries and more dependent upon his own achievements. The woman has more to gain by "marrying up" and more to lose by "marrying down."

For the adolescent girl as well as for the adult woman,

retationships with the opposite sex and those personal qualities which affect the ability to establish such relationships are central in importance. Dating, popularity with boys, pulchritude, "charm," clothes and dancing are preoccupations so central and so obvious that it would be useless pedantry to attempt to document them. The specific content of satisfying and approved relationships with the other sex and the personal attributes which make for success in such relationships may be different in the various ethnic and class subcultures, but always it is within the area of these relationships and these attributes that a girl finds her fulfillments *as a girl*. It is no accident that "boys collect stamps, girls collect boys." There are other areas in which she may find a measure of recognition and satisfaction—as a "career girl," a successful businesswoman, a brilliant student. But her satisfaction is likely to be adulterated if she fails in that area which is specifically symbolic, in her culture, of the female role. She may be compared to the engineer who achieves some gratification from success as an amateur musician but who thinks of himself as first and foremost an engineer, whose overriding aspiration is to be recognized as an engineer and who is judged by the community at large mostly by his performance in the occupation at which he earns his living. He *must* excel in those activities that define the engineer's role.

We should not, therefore, expect the status and the self-evaluation of the girl to be so heavily determined as is the boy's by the middle-class norms we have described. The way in which our culture emphasizes the distinctively masculine character of these virtues is illustrated by a content analysis of third-grade readers:

Perhaps the most striking single finding of this study is the extent to which a differentiation is made between the roles of male and female in the content of these readers ... Female characters, for example, are relatively more frequent among those displaying affiliation, nurturance and harm avoidance. On the other hand, females are less frequent, relatively, among characters displaying activity, aggression, achievement, construction and recognition. Girls and women are thus being shown as sociable, and timid, but inactive, unambitious and uncreative ... In the discussion of passivity it was shown that female characters are portrayed as lazy twice as often, relatively, as male characters. In the discussion of acquisition it was seen that female characters are shown as acquiring in socially disapproved ways much more often, relatively than males, and much less frequently by the approved routes of work and effort ... effort and acquisition of skills are in effect shown as of value only to males.*

From all these considerations we derive two major conclusions. First, the problems of adjustment which we have described at such length in earlier chapters and to which the delinquent subculture is, so to speak, a "tailor-made" solution, are primarily problems of the male role. Second, delinquency of the kind which is institutionalized in the delinquent subculture is *positively inappropriate* as a response to the problems which do arise in the female role. It is inappropriate because it is, at best, irrelevant to the vindication of the girl's status as a girl, and at worst, be-

---

*Irwin L. Child, Elmer H. Potter and Estelle M. Levine, "Children's Textbooks and Personality Development: An Exploration in the Social Psychology of Education," *Psychological Monographs,* LX, No. 3 (1946), pp. 35, 46, 47, 48.

cause it positively threatens her in that status in consequence of its strongly masculine symbolic function.[3]

This is not to deny that delinquency exists among girls
also or even that female delinquency is subcultural. It does,
however, imply that female delinquency is probably motivated by quite different problems than male delinquency
and that the form it takes, whether institutionalized by a
subculture or not, is likely to be different.

We have seen something of the respects in which male
and female delinquency are, in fact, different. The most
conspicuous difference is that male delinquency, particularly the subcultural kind, is versatile, whereas female
delinquency is relatively specialized. It consists overwhelmingly of sexual delinquency or of involvement in
situations that are likely to "spill over" into overt sexuality.
Our task in this volume is to throw light on the delinquent
subculture we have described and not to explain the kind
of delinquency that is characteristically female. On this
large and complex subject we will permit ourselves only
a few observations.

We have said that a female's status, security, response
and the acceptability of her self-image as a woman or a
girl depend upon the establishment of satisfactory relationships with the other sex. To this end sexuality, variously employed, is the most versatile and sovereign single
means. A primary determinant of the female's "peace of
mind" and feeling of security is her assurance of her sexual
attractiveness. It is commonplace that advertising directed
to men makes abundant use of pictures of sexually attractive females. It is more significant for our purpose that the

portrayal of women as relatively undiluted sex objects is probably even more characteristic of advertising directed *to women*. To the man the advertising says: "You may win, perhaps possess and enjoy this sexually attractive and therefore desirable female." To the female it says: "You too may be sexually attractive and therefore successful as a woman or a girl."

Sexual attractiveness must not, of course, be confused with sexual accessibility. Attractiveness alone without accessibility may pay dividends; in the long run it may pay higher dividends. Sexual accessibility, however, has this virtue: it pays the most immediate and certain dividends by way of male attention, male pursuit, male company and the wasteful public expenditure of the male's resources on the female—one of the most socially visible and reassuring evidences of success at the job of being a woman.

At the same time that sexual accessibility has a variety of uses, it has also its costs and its dangers. For the reputation for chastity, however this may be defined in the circles in which the girl moves or to which she aspires, is an important criterion of marriageability and of acceptability as a social equal in "respectable" society. The girl who is "loose" is assured of a male following but weakens her position in the marriage market.

The female equivalent of our "college-boy" must, therefore, also subject herself to a regimen in the interest of the long-run goal of vertical social mobility. Her relationship with a boy, if it is to "pay off" in a "good" marriage or in further movement up the social ladder, via subsequent relationships to higher status males, must be presumed to rest on some other basis than the exchange of male patronage for the dispensation of sexual favors. Along with a reputation for chastity she must cultivate the "style of life"—defined in terms of "charm," "personality," "culture," "breeding" and "taste"—considered desirable for a female in the social level to which she aspires.

With respect to sexuality, it is not repression which is required of her but something perhaps more difficult: the development of skills in the management and husbandry of her sexual resources. She must make shrewd use of her sexuality but must employ it with discretion. She must exploit the possibilities of dieting, "scientific" beauty care and dress to enhance what is usually her most important single asset, and must display her carefully cultivated charms as provocatively as "good taste" will allow. She must, like a magnet, exert an attractive force on male objects; unlike a magnet, she must keep these objects rotating in a narrow orbit around her person without actual contact with them. It is a delicate art but there are many adepts. Training in these skills and the inculcation of the underlying motivation is an important part, we suggest, of middle-class socialization of female children.

The foregoing statement requires some qualification. The definition of "chastity" and "decency" is variable. It does not necessarily exclude the possibility of sexual contact of various degrees and kinds. The *reputation* for chastity may be consistent with contact to the point of consummation. In general, however, the vertically mobile female, if she permits sexual contact, must limit it to the kinds and contexts allowed by current *mores,* and if she exceeds these limits must guard herself against the publicity which would endanger her reputation. Like the college-boy, she must subordinate and discipline affectivity and impulse if she is to "get ahead."

This is an admittedly rudimentary and grossly oversimplified sketch of the uses and hazards of sexuality to the female in our society. There are powerful, socially structured motivations to use overt sexuality for quick dividends; there are powerful countervailing motivations to suppress or control this tendency. It is suggested that the problem of explaining female sex delinquency be viewed as a problem of accounting for choices and compromises between those socially structured alternatives. The determinants of these choices and of their distribution in the various class and ethnic sectors of our role system will not be discussed here. It has been our concern only to show two things: first, that the kind of delinquency we have described under the rubric of the delinquent subculture is not appropriate to the problems of adjustment and the social expectations of the female role; and second, that sex delinquency is *one* kind of meaningful response to the most characteristic, most central and most ego-involved problems of the female role: the establishment of satisfactory relationships with the opposite sex.

THE DELINQUENT SUBCULTURE AND THE DELINQUENT INDIVIDUAL

THE READER might well wonder now: "You have described three different ways of dealing with a certain kind of problem of adjustment. One of these is forming the delinquent subculture you have described. However, you have told us little or nothing about why a particular boy chooses one or another of these various alternatives. Furthermore, what of all the vast literature on the motivation of juvenile delinquency, in particular all the books by psychologists and psychoanalysts? We read there about all sorts of complex and subtle motivations, varying enormously with the problems and circumstances of the child. Does this book propose to make all this literature obsolete!"

The question that this book tries to answer is this: why does a particular subculture, with a certain distinctive content, have its principal locus in a certain role sector in our society? The usual question about delinquency is a different one: why do particular individuals engage in delinquency or participate in the delinquent subculture? It is important that we see clearly why these questions may have different answers.

We have tried to show that a subculture owes its existence to the fact that it provides a solution to certain problems of adjustment shared among a community of individuals. However, it does not follow that for every individual who participates these problems provide the sole or sufficient source of motivation. Indeed, there may be some participants to whose motivation these problems contribute very little.

Consider first that membership, as such, in a social group may yield all sorts of benefits and satisfactions sufficient to motivate people to want to belong. The distinctive creed of such a group may be a matter of indifference to a particular individual; it is not the creed but the other benefits of membership which attract him to the group. Acceptance of that creed, however, may be a condition or by-product of his membership. In such a case, the motivation for his participation in the subculture may throw little light on the reasons for its distinctive content. Conversely, the needs and problems which make intelligible this distinctive content may have little to do with why this particular individual has taken it over.

Let us take a simple example: here is a chapter of the League of Women Voters, an organization whose members share certain understandings, sentiments, and objectives which we may call its subculture. Such an organization with such a subculture could not thrive in this particular community unless there were in this community a group of women whose problems, needs, and interests are such as to motivate them to get together to promote this particular set of objectives. Here, now, is a lady who does not share these problems, needs and interests. However, because her best friend is a member of the League or perhaps bcause membership in such a respectable organization yields a certain increment of status, she also joins and, in consequence of her membership in the organization, comes to take over its subculture. Or perhaps she does share the motivations of the other members but not intensely enough to induce her to join; the fact that her best friend already belongs may suffice to tip the balance of motivation. In either case, her participation is motivated, at least in part, by considerations that have little to do with the content of the subculture itself.

In like manner, we cannot account for the content and locus, within the social system, of the distinctive beliefs and practices we call the Holiness sects without taking account of the distinctive problems of adjustment to which these beliefs and practices answer. Again, however, we may have individuals whose motivation to participate or to prefer this particular solution to their problems would not be complete if participation did not offer other satisfactions which were not directly dependent upon the distinctive content of this particular religion. For one individual, membership offers the possibility to enjoy a position of leadership; another prefers this church because it is convenient; another goes to this church because his customers do and, other things being equal, this makes it preferable to the Baptist church around the corner; still another joins because it is his wife's church and he might as well keep peace in the family.

Our delinquent subculture, by the same token, is not a disembodied set of beliefs and practices but is "carried" and supported by groups with distinctive organization and distinctive personnel. A position in this organization or affiliation with this or that particular member may offer other satisfactions which help to account for the participation of certain members but do not help to explain the content of the culture in which they participate. One boy, for example, may join partly because the delinquent groups in his neighborhood happen to be of his own racial or ethnic in-group, whereas the non-delinquents are predominantly of an out-group from which he wishes to disaffiliate himself as clearly as possible. Another may join a gang as an alternative to being regularly beaten up by that gang.

However, it is quite possible that the motivation to participation may be complicated by considerations of another sort. We have tried to show that the content of the delinquent subculture answers directly to certain problems of adjustment which we have described at great length. It does not follow that the same subculture, or aspects of it, may not at the same time answer directly to other problems as well. What we have described is the *common core* of motivation, widely shared within the social categories from which delinquents are drawn. For certain individuals, motivation may be enhanced because a subculture with this particular content can render other psychological services of which they stand in need. In the language of the psychoanalyst, the motivation of such individuals is "overdetermined."

In the literature of juvenile delinquency we read of "delinquents through a sense of guilt:" persons who harbor strong unconscious feelings of guilt which can be allayed only through some kind of expiation and who turn to crime with an unconscious view to being apprehended and punished. We read of children who have strong unconscious feelings of hostility toward a parent and who, through criminal attacks on substitute parent figures, find some satisfaction of their aggressive drives. We read of others who are beset by some intense anxiety arising out of their uncertainty as to their place in their parents' affections, and who find in delinquency a surcease of anxiety through "flight into activity." There is no need here to review all the functions which delinquency is alleged to perform for this or that individual, or to assess their plausibility. The important thing is to recognize the general principle that almost all things that people do implement not one but several interests of the personality. The human personality is a complex system with many roles, many activities, many aspirations, and therefore many problems. All these aspects of the personality are interdependent, if only because they must all use the same set of arms and legs and must allocate among themselves a finite supply of energy, cash and other resources. Compare it to a family deliberating about what to do with the breadwinner's two week vacation. There are many possibilities, each one of which would suit admirably some interest of some member of the family. But there is only one car, so much time and little money. The ultimate decision is likely to be one which implements a number of different objectives; no one consideration will determine the choice. In like manner the personality, in working out solutions to its problems of adjustment, assesses each potential solution from the standpoint of its serviceability in a number of different problem areas.

The fact, however, that the delinquent subculture may help to solve more than one problem of adjustment does not mean that all such problems must be taken account of in an explanation of that subculture. For it has not been demonstrated, and it seems to us unlikely that it will be demonstrated, that these other problems are distributed in the social system in the same way as the delinquent subculture. They arise on all social levels and in both sexes but it is typically in the male, working-class sector that they find the delinquent subculture rather than some other avenue as their outlet. The reason, as we see it, is this. It is in the male working-class sector that there exists a *common core* of motivation, more specifically, of status discontent, to which the delinquent subculture is an appropriate solution. Over and above this common core there are other problems distributed, each in its own fashion, within the social system. It is this common core, however, which provides the *common ground* for the coalition or joint adventure we call the delinquent gang. The other problems, because they are not likely to be shared by a group of individuals who are in easy and familiar association with one another, cannot give rise to a delinquent subculture. Once such a subculture is established, however, its ability to contribute to the solution of these other problems may well tip the balance in favor of participation for this individual or that.

We have still not exhausted the types of considerations that are relevant on the level of the explanation of the individual case. We have stressed that the delinquent subculture is a joint creation, satisfying to the degree that it is shared with others. This implies that the sheer ecological accessibility of other children with kindred problems may play an important part in the determination of participation. The child's relationships to his family may in various ways facilitate or interpose barriers to such participation. There are broken families, families in which both parents are at work and families which for other reasons are not able to exercise the degree of supervision over the child's associations which may make the difference between participation and non-participation in a delinquent coalition. There are families in which the emotional relationships between the child and his parents are such that the wishes of the parents have little meaning for the child and their approval and disapproval carry little weight as sanctions. In such families the efforts of the parents have little effect as directive or restraining forces on the child's choice of solutions to his problems of adjustment.

If the basic argument of this book, then, is sound, it does not follow that other theories on the "causes of delinquency" are unsound. Our objective is a limited one and one that is different from that of the major literature in this field. We are not primarily interested in explaining why this boy adopts a delinquent solution to his problems and why another boy does not. This is, however, the main preoccupation of the established literature. We make no final assessment of the validity of this or that theory. This book does, however, have implications for the explanation of the individual case. In the first place, at the same time that it recognizes the complexity of individual motivation, it directs attention to one component of motivation which we conceive to be of transcendant importance, the most widely shared and often the most decisive, but a component which is largely ignored by existing theories. In the second place, it emphasizes the role played in the genesis of delinquency, in the "choice of symptom," by accessibility to association with others in search of a solution to *their* problems of adjustment, and this too is a consideration which has received little attention hitherto. In the third place, it insists that the problem of explanation is not disposed of by discovering anxieties, insecurities, men-- tal conflicts, guilt feelings or other problems of adjustment, but that it be convincingly demonstrated that the solution is appropriate to the problem. Not always but far too often the explanation of delinquency stops short with the dem- onstration that the child has problems. To such explana- tions one can only say: "Who doesn't have problems?" And finally, this book suggests that the established theories have tended to locate all the decisive experiences of the child in the family circle and to ignore the world outside the family—the school, the street, the playground, the set- tlement house. This world too is a crucible of personality and a proving ground as well, with its own exacting judges of failure and success.

There is one more matter that must be brought up if not disposed of. The delinquent individual we have been talk- ing about is one who participates in a delinquent subcul- ture. We have not, however, claimed that, even within the working-class male group, all delinquency represents par- ticipation in a delinquent subculture. It seems fairly cer- tain that problems of adjustment do arise which do not lend themselves to such collective delinquent solutions, either because of the peculiar nature of the problems them- selves or because of internal or external barriers to inter- action with similarly circumstanced individuals. Lacking such group support, the delinquent solutions are less likely to arise and some socially less offensive solution is likely to be adopted,[4] but the possibility of a delinquent solution, "contrived" by the individual, is not thereby categorically excluded. Such etiologies have been called "idiosyncratic," "neurotic" and "personal-social." This kind of delinquency is probably far less common than is generally assumed in the professional literature, particularly in the psychiatrically oriented literature, but its existence cannot lightly be denied.

The reader may protest that even if this kind of delinquency constitutes a relatively small fraction of all delinquent behavior, there is no justification for complacency and that the task of explaining it cannot be shrugged off on the grounds of the numbers involved. The task of social policy is to cope with delinquency whatever its roots. The task of science is unceasingly to scrutinize, revise and refine our theories so that they encompass more and more of the total field of delinquent behavior, subcultural and otherwise. We agree. The limitation of the subject matter of the present volume to subcultural delinquency is a matter of convenience only. We do not disparage the importance of the problems which are left untreated.

Despite the fact, however, that our present concern is with subcultural delinquency, it seems appropriate to remark that the way in which we state the problems of personal-social or non-cultural delinquency is not unaffected by the perspective provided by this volume. We have repeatedly observed that the psychiatric literature on juvenile delinquency, which constitutes the greater bulk of that literature, has often tended to treat delinquency as a simple function of the actor's problems of adjustment. Cultural support and legitimation of particular solutions have, on the whole, either been ignored or treated as relatively unimportant or auxiliary or countervailing forces to the pressures from within the individual. Contemporary social-psy-chological research, on the other hand, has accumulated a large body of evidence to the effect that the human actor, in working out solutions to his problems, seeks such support and legitimation; lacking it, his solutions are either imperfect or not solutions at all. Our own theory is an effort to find an explanation of delinquency which is consistent with this new knowledge. If this new knowledge is sound, however, we are now faced with this question. *How is it possible* for an individual to contrive a solution which is wholly lacking in social support, which is not validated by consensus and not rewarded by satisfying human relations? How is it possible for an individual to "go it alone?" To what extent are the exceptions but seeming exceptions and, to the extent that they are truly exceptions, what are the circumstances under which they occur and what are the mechanisms which make them possible? The congruence of the actor's solutions with those institutionalized in his milieu can no longer be regarded simply as a datum, to be recorded when it is present and ignored when it is absent. The failure of such congruence is itself a problem and demands explanation in its own right.

MIDDLE-CLASS DELINQUENCY

IT IS NOT enough that our theory—or any other theory—should account plausibly for gang delinquency among working-class boys. It must ultimately come to terms with the facts of middle-class delinquency as well. This may amount, to be sure, to but a fraction of working-class delinquency. However, the middle-class parents whose son "gets in trouble" will surely take small comfort in the knowledge that the delinquency rate for children of their social class is relatively small. Furthermore, from the scientific point of view, middle-class delinquency is a body of data with which any theory of juvenile delinquency must be consistent. Until this consistency can be established, middle-class delinquency remains a continual source of embarrassment to those who would defend the theory.

Insofar as the delinquency we find in the middle class is subcultural in nature and fits the description of working-class subcultural delinquency, it throws into question the thesis of this book. The explanation we have offered assumes that the delinquent subculture is the outgrowth of conditions which are typically working-class. If it should turn out that the same phenomenon can flourish independently of those conditions, it would strongly suggest that those conditions are not necessary *even in the working class*. It would suggest that we may have overlooked some other constellation of circumstances which also makes sense of the delinquent subculture and which can be found in both the working class and the middle class.

However, if we may, for the moment, speculate without committing ourselves, there are several other possibilities. First, it is possible that the circumstances which, according to our theory, give rise to the delinquent subculture may sometimes be found in families which, *from the standpoint of purely economic criteria of social class,* would ordinarily be considered middle-class. It will be remembered, however, that the most crucial elements of our

explanation relate not so much to the income and the economic disadvantage of the working class as to aspects of
family culture and methods of child rearing which bear a
strong but by no means perfect relationship to income and
occupation. We have already remarked that many families
which are working-class in terms of income and occupation
are middle-class in terms of culture. By the same token,
many families which are middle-class in economic terms
and live in what are known as middle-class neighborhoods
may be decidedly working-class in terms of the experiences
they provide their children. Not only the working class
but all social classes, if we define them in economic terms
alone, are culturally heterogeneous. Wherever we find
the cultural conditions called for by our theory, we may
expect to find the soil for the delinquent subculture. It is
conceivable, then, that much of the delinquency found in
"over-privileged" neighborhoods may be the same, in
terms of both content and etiology, as the delinquency
with which we have been concerned in this book.

Another possibility is that the same delinquent subculture arises in the working class and the middle class in
response to different but "functionally equivalent" sets
of conditions. That is, we cannot reject out of hand the
possibility that life in the middle class systematically generates problems of adjustment different from those in the
working class but nonetheless problems to which the same
subcultural solutions are appropriate. We do not, however, regard this as *probable* because it is one of the lessons of modern social science that culture patterns are seldom duplicated in radically different social contexts; sel-

dom does a pattern, "tailor-made" to fit the characteristic life-problems of one group, fit, without alteration, the problems of another.

It seems to us more likely that subcultural delinquency in the different social classes will prove to be kin but by no means identical twins. We would anticipate that subcultural delinquency in the middle class will turn out to differ in quality as well as frequency from that which we found in the working class; that is, subcultural delinquency in the different social classes is a qualitatively different response to qualitatively different problems arising in different contexts of communication and interaction. We surmise, however, that there are certain strands of motivation that will characterize the male role on both social levels, as a result of which the patterns of delinquency on those levels will bear to one another a certain family resemblance.

This section of the book is frankly a speculative toying with possibilities. This is because we are sadly lacking in solid research concerning the content and substance of middle-class delinquency. In Chapter II we concluded that there is good scientific evidence of a large difference in the *volume* of delinquency between the social classes. There has been hardly any research, however, on the respects, if any, in which delinquency on the different social levels differs in content, other than a couple of articles by Wattenberg and Balistrieri, which contain some suggestive material. In one study* they found that gang member-

---

*William W. Wattenberg and James J. Balistrieri, "Gang Membership and Juvenile Misconduct," *American Sociological Review*, XV (December, 1950), 744-752.

ship was more frequent among delinquents from substandard homes and racially mixed neighborhoods. In another study* they found that, compared to all boys in trouble, boys apprehended for automobile theft were more likely to come from neighborhoods rated "above average" by the police and less likely to come from neighborhoods rated as slums. Why this should be is by no means clear, but it does suggest the possiblity that there may be other respects as well in which the pattern of delinquency may vary with socio-economic status. It is possible that these other differences, if they exist, may not all be readily determined from inspection of official delinquency records, which are usually meager with respect to the concrete details of the delinquency. It is noteworthy that, despite the findings of the first study, Wattenberg and Balistrieri found that the automobile-theft group were somewhat more likely than the rest of their sample "to be members of definite gangs with a reputation of either being rambunctious or engaging in organized theft,"† which suggests that this automobile theft was part of a well established subculture.

In any case, until we have more descriptive knowledge about middle-class delinquency, how it resembles and how it differs from working-class delinquency, we can do little more than speculate about its causes and its implications for the views advanced in this book.

---

*William W. Wattenberg and James J. Balistrieri, "Automobile Theft: A 'Favored-Group' Delinquency," *American Journal of Sociology*, LVII (May, 1952), 575-579.

†*Ibid.*, p. 577.

Talcott Parsons* has offered an extremely interesting and plausible perspective on juvenile delinquency which is especially relevant in the present context. Although his view has not yet had much impact on the literature of criminology and juvenile delinquency, it may provide the key to the understanding of middle-class delinquency. It should be emphasized that Parsons advances this view as an explanation of delinquency *in general;* however, it seems to us that the circumstances to which he attributes delinquency are most marked in the middle class.

In brief, Parsons argues that in our society the mother is the most important agent for socialization and the transmission of the traditional canons of good behavior. The mother's special role results from the fact that the modern urban family tends to be small; that the conjugal unit of father, mother and minor children tends to be residentially and otherwise isolated from related conjugal units; that the child at best has close emotional relationships with very few adults other than his parents; and that, because of the nature of our complex and highly technical division of labor, because of the father's preoccupation with a "job" of which the young child is likely to have little awareness or understanding, and because of the father's pursuit of his occupation for long hours in a factory, shop or office remote from the home, the child is likely to perceive his mother as the principal exemplar of morality, source of discipline and object of identification.

---

*Talcott Parsons, "Certain Primary Sources and Patterns of Aggression in the Social Structure of the Western World," *Psychiatry*, X (May, 1947), 167-181.

These generalizations are true for young children of both sexes. They have different implications for boys and girls, however. Girls are expected to grow up to be like their mothers; boys are expected to become "manly" like their fathers. Both children have tended to form a direct feminine identification. For the girl this tendency is consistent with later expectations and demands upon her. Femininity comes to her easily and naturally. Her conception of herself as a girl is not threatened by impulses to identify with male figures or to behave in ways that are not expressive of her sex role. The boy, however, has no comparable calm assurance that he is indubitably, in his own eyes and those of the world around him, a representative and recognizable specimen of his sex. He knows it is shameful for a boy to be like a woman and he feels constrained to rebel against all those impulses which he feels might be suggestive of femininity and to exaggerate all those traits which set him apart from the other sex.

In addition to the mother's being the object of love and identification, she is to the young boy the principal agent of socially significant discipline. Not only does she administer the disciplines which make him a tolerable citizen of the family group, but she stimulates him to give a good account of himself outside the home and makes known her disappointment and disapproval if he fails to measure up to her expectations. She, above all, focuses in herself the symbols of what is "good" behavior, of conformity with the expectations of the adult respectable world. When he revolts against identification with his mother in the name of masculinity, it is not surprising that a boy unconsciously identifies "goodness" with femininity and that being a "bad boy" becomes a positive goal . . . there is a strong tendency for boyish behavior to run in anti-social if not directly destructive directions, in striking contrast to that of pre-adolescent girls.*

Summarizing: Because of the structure of the modern family and the nature of our occupational system, children of both sexes tend to form early feminine identifications. The boy, however, unlike the girl, comes later under strong social pressure to establish his masculinity, his *difference from* female figures. Because his mother is the object of the feminine identification which he feels is the threat to his status as a male, he tends to react negativistically to those conduct norms which have been associated with mother and therefore have acquired feminine significance. Since mother has been the principal agent of indoctrination of "good," respectable behavior, "goodness" comes to symbolize femininity, and engaging in "bad" behavior acquires the function of denying his femininity and therefore asserting his masculinity. This is the motivation to juvenile delinquency.

Of course Parsons has not been the first to emphasize the role of the "masculine protest" in generating aggressive and "antisocial" behavior.[5] The novel and distinctively sociological element in his treatment of the subject is the linkage of the "masculine protest" motif to certain aspects of the structure of modern society, especially the family and occupational systems. We may, however, go a step farther. There is reason to believe that all the characteristics which Parsons attributes to the social world in which the modern male child grows up are accentuated in the social world of the middle-class child. The small family

Ibid., p. 172.

and the isolation from socially significant adults other than the parents are most typically middle-class. The probability that the child has no opportunity to see the father in his occupational role and that that role will be unintelligible to the child is stronger in the middle class. The probability that the father *at home* engages in distinctively and visibly masculine activities sharply contrasting to those of the mother is greater in the working class. We suggest that, because of the greater freedom of movement of the working-class child inside and outside the neighborhood, and because working-class neighborhoods are more likely to be mixed residential-commercial-industrial neighborhoods, the working-class child is more likely to see within the area of his normal daily movements the distinctive activities of men and women, and therefore to build up definitions of masculinity which are positive and independent and not merely negations of femininity. The working-class male child, furthermore, is more likely from the very beginning to have clearly defined for him, by his parents, his neighbors and his peers, his sex role and the distinctive patterns of behavior which go with it and to be systematically rewarded for assuming characteristically masculine behavior. For all these reasons, we would expect the working-class boy to make an earlier masculine identification, to have less anxiety about his masculinity, to have a richer and more positive conception of the meaning of masculinity than the mere antithesis of "goodness," and therefore that he is not so likely to resort to "badness" simply as a device to prove to himself and the world that he is really masculine.[6]

We suggest that the problem of achieving an assured sense of masculinity is further aggravated in the middle-class by the prolonged dependence of the child upon his parents into and often beyond his 'teens and by the indefinite postponement of an adult and unequivocally masculine role. For the girl, a state of dependence upon others and the postponement of economic self-sufficiency and of self-determination in general, while irritating, perhaps, are not likely to disturb her self-conception *as a girl*. For the boy, a prolonged period of tutelage, of dependence upon his parents, of schooling in *preparation for* a job which may materialize in a remote and indefinite future, are much more likely to make him feel insecure in his sex role. For the working-class boy, the hiatus between childhood dependency and adult self-determination is much briefer, emancipation from controls of both mother and father comes more quickly, the opportunity to engage in an earnest and not a token manner in activities of adult males and thereby to test and to affirm his maleness comes earlier. If the middle-class boy earns money in occasional or steady "jobs," his family is very likely to look benevolently and approvingly upon his "jobs" as "good training" but his earnings are not as vital to the family coffers as are those of the working-class boy. The earnings of the working-class boy, in other words, are more likely to be regarded in the same light as those of his father; he really shares the "breadwinner" role. In brief, not only must the middle-class boy overcome an early feminine identification and prove his maleness; even the opportunities to assume the legitimate signs of maleness are likely to be denied him.

Something of the flavor of the kinds of circumstances which encourage a masculine identification untroubled by doubts and anxieties is suggested in the following excerpt from an autobiographical document by a male college student:

All of us had our prescribed work and chores to do which kept us busy. My particular chores were made enjoyable because part of the garden and part of the animals were my own, the proceeds of which I could keep. I was also aware of the fact that I was helping to feed a big family. This, I remember, gave me the greatest satisfaction. . . . My father encouraged my participation in sports, bought uniforms, gloves, bats, balls, usually with my own money, and helped me organize a baseball team. He helped me train my dogs to hunt, showed me how to "run a trap line," showed me the best fishing and hunting methods. He helped me build a bank account through the sale of pelts, chickens, eggs, and through raising rabbits, pigeons and guinea pigs.

This is, of course, a portrait of a rural rather than an urban working-class background. Some of the details, for example, the emphasis on saving, are more typically middle-class than working-class. The features of this portrait, however, which tend to establish an early and secure masculine self-conception are, on the whole, more likely to occur in working-class than in middle-class families.

It seems to us that the sex-role anxieties and the masculine protest, arising out of the circumstances described by Parsons and aggravated by the considerations we have added, might well provide a basis for a coming-together of children who share these problems and for the creation of a jointly supported delinquent subculture. To Parsons' formulation we would add that the circumstances which motivate this masculine protest are most typically to be found in the middle-class and that the explanation, therefore, is most relevant to middle-class delinquency.

It will be remembered that we argued in a previous section that aggressive, exploitative and destructive behavior commended itself to working-class boys also, because of the strongly masculine symbolic significance such behavior has acquired in our culture. If, then, Parsons' thesis, as modified by us, is correct, there is an important common thread of motivation running through both working-class and middle-class delinquency. As we see it, however, male delinquency in families which are culturally middle-class is *primarily* an attempt to cope with a basic anxiety in the area of sex-role identification; it has the primary function of giving reassurance of one's essential masculinity. The motivation to working-class delinquency is more complicated. The *primary* problem of adjustment is in the area of ego-involved status differences in a status system defined by the norms of respectable middle-class society. The delinquent subculture of the working class boy has the primary functions: first, of establishing a set of status criteria in terms of which the boy can more easily succeed; and second, of enabling him to retaliate against the norms at whose impact his ego has suffered, by defining merit in terms of the opposite of those norms and by sanctioning aggression against them and those who exemplify and apply them. The fact that this behavior is symbolic of masculinity heightens the appeal of this response because it is consistent with his conception of himself as a male and because there are few other avenues of distinctively masculine achievement open to him which are also instrumental to the solution of his status problems. It also helps to explain why girls do not resort to this kind of behavior. The heart of the matter may be expressed in this way: the working-class boy has his problem of adjustment and his motivation to the formation of a delinquent subculture even if his masculinity is not threatened by an early feminine identificaton; the middle-class boy has his problem in the area of sex-role identification and a motivation to being "bad" even if he is equipped to succeed in the area in which the working-class boy is handicapped.

We make no attempt here to explore exhaustively this problem of middle-class delinquency. How pervasive and how intense are these problems of achieving masculinity? In what ways are working-class and middle-class delinquency alike and in what ways different? What countervailing pressures are there in the middle-class to the adoption of this mode of masculine protest? All these questions require further research. We have sketched out some theoretical leads and have suggested, in this section and in that which follows, some directions which research might take.

THE FUTURE OF RESEARCH

THE MORAL of these last few pages is that this book is a prolegomenon and a signpost to further research as well as a tentative solution to a major theoretical problem. Monographs on juvenile delinquency are many and voluminous, the periodical literature is prolific and the statistics accumulate interminably. The sufficiency of the data, however, is always relative to the questions we ask and the answers

we seek to verify. We have tried, in this book, to develop
a theory consistent with the "known facts" about the delinquent subculture. It is remarkable, however, how insuffi-
cient are these "known facts" for the conclusive validation
or further modification of this theory. This is partly due,
no doubt, to the inherent difficulty of obtaining the necessary data, but partly also to the fact that the data at hand
have been gathered with other objectives, theoretical and
practical, in mind. It is appropriate, we think, to consider
the kinds of research necessary for a better understanding
of the delinquent subculture and, indeed, of delinquency
in general.

First and foremost, we must overcome the limitations
inherent in all official or quasi-official data on juvenile
delinquency. The defect of these data, of course, is not
that they represent too small a sample but that we cannot
tell what sorts of delinquents and delinquencies may be
overrepresented or underrepresented. We can never lay
to rest the ghost of unrepresentativeness as long as our
statistical base of operations is delinquencies known to the
courts, the police, or even the schools and the social agencies. Until this defect is remedied, comparisons between
delinquents and non-delinquents with respect to their
developmental histories, personalities and social position
must be received with some scepticism and reserve. In
order to remedy this defect, we must start, not with known
delinquents, but with *representative samples of the juvenile population* drawn without regard to their known or
probable delinquent histories. *Then,* on the basis of interviews, questionnaires and tests we must differentiate these

samples into delinquents and non-delinquents of various degrees and kinds. In this manner alone can we achieve a valid conception of the distribution, by degree and kind, of delinquency within sectors and strata of the population.

This has never been done.[7] On the basis of his own and others' experience it is the conviction of the author that it can be done. It has been argued that it is difficult to approach a sample of children, not selected with reference to their known delinquent histories, and elicit from them full and frank accounts of delinquencies hitherto unknown and unsuspected. This difficulty must be reckoned with but is exaggerated. The author and other investigators have found that with proper "build-up" and insurance of anonymity, school children are remarkably willing to speak freely of their delinquencies. Extraordinary ingenuity and resources have been invested in research foredoomed to inconclusive results because the point of departure has been a group of known delinquents to which a group of presumed non-delinquents has been matched, rather than a *representative group of children* to be subsequently differentiated into delinquent and non-delinquent. The kind of research suggested here would certainly not cost any more or require any greater methodological ingenuity.[8]

Our second suggestion concerns an altered emphasis in the kinds of information sought. Research in delinquency has always been overwhelmingly preoccupied with "correlates" of delinquency: life-histories, family backgrounds, personality characteristics as revealed by interviews, personality and neurotic inventories and case studies. It is not our intention to minimize the importance of this kind

of information. It is striking, however, how perfunctory
has been our concern with the delinquent action itself, that
with which these "correlates" are presumably correlated.
In what passes for a "thorough" report on a delinquent
child, we can often learn more about his pre-natal care
and the condition of his teeth than about his delinquent
behavior itself. The assumption seems to be common that
delinquency, like measles, is a homogeneous something
that people either have or have not and that it is sufficient,
therefore, simply to note that a person either is or is not
a "delinquent." More refined analysis may note that the
person has committed "many" or "few" delinquencies and
that these delinquencies include "sex offenses," "stealing,"
"truancy," "running away," "ungovernability," and a few
other categories borrowed from legal usage and statistical
compilations.

We believe that an adequate understanding of delinquency and of delinquent subcultures cannot be grounded
upon such meager and superficial data. The validity of
our own explanation is contingent upon the accuracy of
our description of the delinquent subculture and the validity of any explanation is contingent upon its consistency
with the details of the data it purports to explain. The anal-
ogy of delinquency to a "symptom" meriting little investigation in its own right has been much overworked. If we
wish to retain it, however, we would do well to remember
that physicians, from whose vocabulary the term is borrowed, do not lump together fevers, rashes, boils, aches
and pains, jaundice, vertigo and spots before the eyes as
"symptoms," differences among which may be safely ig-

nored. The syphilis spirochete is not considered a satisfactory explanation for violent sneezing in the month of August. For the understanding of delinquency as well we must discover the significant respects in which this behavior may vary, describe our delinquents in terms of these dimensions of variation, and construct our theories to fit the richness and particularity of the data.

This means that we need much more full and detailed data on the delinquent action itself. We need to know more about the frequency, the variety, the sequences and the spacing of delinquency in the child's history; about the "spirit," the "quality," the "emotional tone" of the delinquent action; about the circumstances, events, and activities which provide the context preceding, accompanying and following the delinquent act; and above all, we need to know more about the collective or individual nature of the delinquent act and how delinquency varies in individual and group situations. With such information at our disposal, we can construct typologies and other classificatory schemes which will enable us better to describe variations in our data and relate those variations to variations in personal characteristics, life histories, and age, sex, ethnic, social class and other role positions.

Lastly, it would be desirable to continue and expand research on delinquent groups as social systems, that is, research whose object is the structure, the processes, the history and the subculture of the group as such rather than the delinquent individual. A valuable start has been made but much remains to be done. Such research should investigate systematically the origin and dissolution of these groups, their status systems, their spirit and ideologies, their systems for control and maintenance of morale and their attitudes toward and interaction with other agencies and groups in the wider community. It should investigate the processes of mutual exploration and tentative inter-action between the gang and non-gang members and how they lead to recruitment, rejection or withdrawal. As in the study of the delinquent individual, we should be concerned with *variation* in all these respects, especially in the content of their subcultures and status systems, in order that we may have a fuller awareness of those per-mutations in our data which our theories do *not* fit as well as those which they seem plausibly to explain. Needless to say, this type of research is fraught with great difficulty. Our techniques for the study of small groups in action are crude and the problems of "getting close" to live delin-quent groups and observing them at first hand are enor-mous. On the other hand, no type of research is of poten-tially greater value for throwing new light on delinquency and the challenge is worth all the ingenuity we can muster.

DELINQUENCY CONTROL

A WORD is necessary for the reader who is impatient for solutions to the social problems of prevention and treat-ment. If things are as we have described them, then what ought we to do?

The reader's impatience is understandable. Progress in the control of juvenile delinquency, if at all discernible, has certainly not been spectacular. One justification of an inquiry into causes is to suggest more effective remedies.

If we have succeeded in this volume in revealing more clearly some of the social origins of juvenile delinquency, surely this new understanding must have implications for social policy.

However, drawing morals and laying down precepts is a serious business. From a diagnosis of a social ill, even a correct one, the "right" solution does not leap to the eye in any direct and obvious way. Compare delinquency with malaria. We know the causes of the disease. We know the responsible microorganism and its life cycle. We know the mosquito that carries it and we know its habits. We know the conditions which breed the mosquito. This knowledge suggests the directions in which to seek for solutions. It suggests various strategic points at which we might enter the circle of causation. We might try to change the conditions which breed the mosquito. We might try to exterminate the mosquitos before they can reach the human victim. We might try to erect barriers to contact between the mosquito and the victim. We might rely on drugs which confer resistance or aid recovery. But each of these possibilities raises new questions. Are all these things possible, and if so, by what means? The answers to these questions are not magically given once we know the causes of the disease. Assuming, however, that we can have the requisite technical knowledge, that we know which of these things can be done and how they can be done, what then? Each of these solutions entails costs and encounters resistances. They may require organized community effort and the expenditure of community resources, which in turn may require either voluntary cooperation or compulsory participation. They may require all manner of sacrifices, changes in established habits, the dissemination of new knowledge and the transformation of old values. The "best" approach or combination of approaches may well be different from the point of view of different segments of the population because the costs of these approaches, in terms of material expenditures and violence to traditional sentiments and habits, may be different from the point of view of each of these different segments. There are no neat and simple syllogisms which lead us directly and unequivocally from the cause to the "correct" policy.

Now consider delinquency. In this volume we have set forth some rather specific ideas about the causation of the delinquent subculture. We have not explained this subculture as a consequence of some particular concrete circumstance but as the consequence of whole webs and chains of circumstances. We have mentioned a number of things which may be considered aspects of the "cause" in the sense that, were they different, the outcome would be different. It follows that, if we want to change the outcome, these are the things we might want to control.

However, as in the case of malaria, this is only the beginning. Of these various circumstances and features of our social system which are involved in the production of the delinquent subculture, which are subject to deliberate control? From the purely technical standpoint, exactly how is it possible to manipulate them in accordance with our wishes. How, for example, can we enable the working-class male to compete more effectively for status in a largely middle-class world or, if we want to cut into the web of causation at another point, how can we change the norms of the middle-class world so that his working-class characteristics do not relegate him to an inferior status? *If* these things are possible, we must then ask: What price are we willing to pay for this or that change? Since any social system is a complex network of inter-dependencies, any change designed to effect a reduction of delinquency may have all sorts of ramifying conse-quences. What consequences may we anticipate and are we willing to accept them? Many teachers, for example, are intuitively aware of the dilemma: to reward the "meritorious" and implicitly humiliate the handicapped, or to abandon this system of competition and invidious discrim-ination and abandon therewith a most powerful spur to the development of the kind of character most of us so highly prize. Or need we not contend with such agonizing dilemmas? Is this dilemma, perhaps, a spurious one, or can we enter the web at some other point, where we may obtain as effective results at a lesser cost to traditional values and interests? In any case, the formulation of policy is a matter of choosing among alternatives and our choices must involve not only technical considerations but the bal-ancing of social values.

Drawing inferences for policy from a theory about the causes of delinquency is, then, a complex and difficult affair and entails a certain social responsibility. It calls for reasoning as careful and disciplined as an inquiry into causes, and a sensitivity to the diverse values which may be at stake. It is not an occasion for leaping to casual or ill-considered conclusions. We do hope that in this volume we have cleared a way to fresh and constructive thinking about problems of delinquency control. We are not prepared to issue pronouncements and we are not at all sure where the road might lead.

CONCLUSION

THIS BOOK is an attempt to formulate and to solve certain neglected but crucial problems. Most of the literature in the field of juvenile delinquency is concerned with the question: why does this or that boy become delinquent? But if we look at the facts of delinquency in their life setting, we do not see so many boys, each becoming a delinquent after his fashion, or severally after the same fashion. We see, for the most part, gangs of boys *doing things together*: sitting on curbs, standing on the corner, going to the movies, playing ball, smashing windows and "goin' robbin'." These things they do are not the simultaneous expression and magical coincidence of so many discrete impulses, each with its own history, each fully understandable apart from the others. They are joint activities, deriving their meaning and flavor from the fact of togetherness and governed by a set of common understandings, common sentiments, and common loyalties. How do these understandings, sentiments and loyalties—what we have called the group's subculture—arise and become the property of the group? Why do these subcultures have the content they do, and why do groups with such subcultures flourish most in certain parts of our population? Perhaps it is sufficient justification of the present work to have put these questions bluntly.

We have attempted also in these pages to answer these questions in a way which will be consistent with the available knowledge about juvenile delinquency and about the structure of American society. It is assumed that future research may reveal defects in this theory. Whatever the outcome of that research, this book will have served a purpose. It will have stimulated thinking and research along new lines leading, we hope, to a fuller and clearer descriptive knowledge of the facts we are trying to explain, to the further reconstruction of theory, and ultimately to a better understanding of juvenile delinquency in our society.

Notes

CHAPTER I

1. A classic statement of this "cultural-transmission" theory of juvenile delinquency is contained in Clifford R. Shaw and Henry D. McKay, *Social Factors in Juvenile Delinquency*, Vol. II of National Commission on Law Observance and Enforcement, *Report on the Causes of Crime* (Washington: U. S. Government Printing Office, 1931). In this volume the "delinquency areas" of the city of Chicago are described and the persistence of juvenile delinquency in those areas is attributed to the persistence of a delinquent tradition or culture. In a later volume, *Juvenile Delinquency in Urban Areas* (Chicago: University of Chicago Press, 1942), Shaw and McKay describe and interpret the distribution of juvenile delinquency in twenty American cities from the same point of view. Ruth Topping, "Treatment of the Pseudo-Social Boy," *American Journal of Orthopsychiatry*, XIII (April, 1943), 353-360 and Frank Tannenbaum, *Crime and the Community* (Boston: Ginn and Company, 1938) are well known expositions of cultural-transmission views. The late Edwin H. Sutherland's "theory of differential association" is a general theory of criminal behavior couched in what are essentially cultural-transmission terms. See Chapter I of his *Principles of Criminology* (4th ed.; Philadelphia: J. B. Lippincott Company, 1947).

2. This is, of course, the most simple, uncomplicated kind of orthodox Freudian explanation. It is stated in a very forthright way in the following quotation from one of the basic works of psychoanalytical criminology, Franz Alexander and Hugo Staub, *The Criminal, the Judge and the Public: A Psychological Analysis* (New York: The MacMillan Company), pp. 34-35:

> However, within the innermost nucleus of the personality ... it is impossible to differentiate normal from criminal impulses. The human being enters the world as a criminal, *i.e.*, socially not adjusted. During the first years of his life the human individual preserves his criminality to the fullest degree. . . . The criminal carries out in his actions his natural, unbridled, instinctual drives; he acts as the child would act if it only could. The repressed, and therefore unconscious criminality of the normal man finds a few socially harmless outlets, like the dream and phantasy of life, neurotic symptoms and also some transitional forms of behavior

which are harmless. . . . The only difference between the criminal and the normal individual is that the normal man partially controls his criminal drives and finds outlets for them in socially harmless activities.

If we start with such a conception of human nature, then our problem is not to explain crime but rather its absence. As another analyst puts it: "We must now ask what, if any, are the reasons why some individuals have enough of inhibitory mechanisms to refrain from transgressions while others lack these prohibitory functions?" David Abrahamsen, *Crime and the Human Mind* (New York: Columbia University Press, 1944), p. 135.

Kate Friedlander, in a recent treatise on juvenile delinquency, develops an elaborate classification of types of juvenile delinquency, basic to which is the assumption of the "antisocial character formation," which is the consequence of "the strength of unmodified instinctive urges, the weakness of the ego, and the lack of independence of the superego." *The Psycho-analytical Approach to Juvenile Delinquency: Theory: Case Studies: Treatment* (New York: International Universities Press, 1947), pp. 94, 184-187. See also, by the same author, "Formation of the Antisocial Character," in *The Psychoanalytical Study of the Child, Vol. I* (New York: International Universities Press, 1945), pp.190-191.

Richard L. Jenkins offers another variant of this approach. He recognizes three types of personalities found in problem children; each is distinguished by the nature of the

"shell of inhibition" which contains the core of primitive unsocialized impulses. Type III, the "socialized delinquent," possesses a normal shell of inhibition *towards members of an in-group,* but towards members of any out-group there is a deficit in the inhibitions. Type III, it is important to note, is not the same as the delinquent as conceived by Shaw, Sutherland and others. What the child has learned in social interaction is not the pattern of delinquency itself but a peculiar superego which disciplines only those delinquent impulses which are directed against the gang. See Richard L. Jenkins, "Psychiatric Interpretations and Considerations of Treatment," in Lester E. Hewitt and Richard L. Jenkins (eds.), *Fundamental Patterns of Maladjustment* (published by The State of Illinois, no date), pp. 81-89, and Richard L. Jenkins, "A Psychiatric View of Personality Structure in Children," in *Yearbook, National Probation Association, 1943* (New York: National Probation Association, 1944), pp. 199-217.

3. One of the most influential statements of this point of view by writers of a generally psychoanalytical persuasion is William Healy and Augusta F. Bronner, *New Light on Delinquency and its Treatment* (New Haven: Yale University Press, 1936). An important treatise, fairly well divorced from psychoanalytical preconceptions, is D. H. Stott, *Delinquency and Human Nature* (Dumferline, Fife: The Carnegie United Kingdom Trust, 1950). Chapters on delinquency in almost any general textbook in clinical psychology are written predominantly

from this point of view. They emphasize (in common with psychoanalysis and psychiatry generally) the idea of delinquency as an attempt at problem-solving through the use of the various mechanisms of adjustment but do not, as a rule, commit the authors to the special conception of the instinctual life and of invariant stages of personality development which characterize the psychoanalytical system of thought. It is to be noted that the contribution of psychoanalysts to the understanding of juvenile delinquency is not to be judged only by the formal, explicit statements of psychoanalytical theory to be found in their general and summary chapters. Many readers will find that the case histories written by psychoanalysts often contain insights and interpretations which are illuminating and persuasive but which have only a tenuous connection with the writers' formal theoretical position. All orthodox psychoanalysts, for example, subscribe to a complicated set of ideas about the fundamental role of "the instincts," but the validity and the value of many of their arguments do not depend upon the validity of this set of ideas. See, for example, the following classics of psychoanalytical criminology: August Aichorn, *Wayward Youth* (New York: The Viking Press, 1935) and Franz Alexander and William Healy *Roots of Crime* (New York: Alfred A. Knopf, 1935).

4. See the table of criminal types in Franz Alexander and Hugo Staub, *op. cit.*, pp. 145-152, especially the "normal, non-neurotic criminal whose Super-Ego is criminal," p. 148. All of the psychoanalytical

writers we have mentioned acknowledge the relevance of "the social factor," but they tend to see it as a circumstance which triggers or precipitates a delinquent impulse which is already fully formed but "latent." Friedlander, for example, cites the case of "Billy," who committed his earlier offences only in the company of older delinquents. But "Billy was attracted by this type of boy because such boys behaved as he wished to behave . . . We can therefore say that the prevalence of rough boys in a neighborhood increases the temptation and is another secondary factor likely to change latent into manifest delinquency, but it is not a causative factor in delinquent behavior." Kate Friedlander, *The Psychoanalytical Approach . . .*, pp. 107-108. See also Franz Alexander and William Healy, *op. cit.*, pp. 275, 282; William Healy and Augusta F. Bronner, *op. cit.*, pp. 50 ff.; August Aichorn, *op. cit.*, pp. 40-41. On the other hand we have psychoanalysts like Fritz Redl, whose versatility and originality are not amenable to the discipline of any established system of thought. In his writing, the notion of a delinquent who is acting out a positive morality—not an instinctive impulse—which is group-derived and group-supported occupies not a peripheral but a very central position. See his "The Psychology of Gang Formation and the Treatment of Juvenile Delinquents," in *The Psychoanalytic Study of the Child, Vol. I* (New York: International Universities Press, 1945), pp. 367-377.

5. See, for example, in addition to the typology by Alexander and

Staub (note 4 above), the following: Alfred R. Lindesmith and H. Warren Dunham, "Some Principles of Criminal Typology," *Social Forces*, XIX (March, 1941), 307-314; J. F. Brown and Douglas W. Orr, "The Field-Theoretical Approach to Criminology," *Journal of Criminal Psychopathology*, III (October, 1941), 236-252; Walter W. Argon, "A Proposed Functional Classification of Criminal Behavior," *Journal of Criminal Psychopathology*, IV (April, 1943), 687-701.

CHAPTER II

1. See H. M. Tiebout and M. E. Kirkpatrick, "Psychiatric Factors in Stealing," *American Journal of Orthopsychiatry*, II (April, 1932), 114-123, which discusses, in an exceptionally lucid manner, the distinction between motivating factors which center around the acquisition of the object and those which center around the commission of the act itself.

The non-utilitarian nature of juvenile delinquency has been noted by many students. ". . . while older offenders may have definitely crystallized beliefs about profitable returns from anti-social conduct, it is very clear that in childhood and in earlier youth delinquency is certainly not entered into as a paying proposition in any ordinary sense." William Healy and Augusta F. Bronner, *op. cit.*, p. 22. "The juvenile property offender's thefts, at least at the start, are usually 'for fun' and not for gain." Paul Tappan, *Juvenile Delinquency* (New York: McGraw Hill Book Company, 1949), p. 143. "Stealing, the leading predatory activity of the adolescent gang, is as much a result of the sport motive as of a desire for revenue." Frederic M. Thrasher, *The Gang* (Chicago: University of Chicago Press, 1936), p. 143. "In its early stages, delinquency is clearly a form of play." Henry D. McKay, "The Neighborhood and Child Conduct," *Annals of the American Academy of Political and Social Science*, CCLXI (January, 1949), 37. See also Barbara Bellow, Milton L. Blum, Kenneth B. Clark, *et al.*, "Prejudice in Seaside," *Human Relations*, I (1947), 15-16 and Sophia M. Robison, Nathan Cohen and Murray Sachs, "An Unsolved Problem in Group Relations," *Journal of Educational Psychology*, XX (November, 1946), 154-162. The last cited paper is an excellent description of the non-utilitarian, malicious and negativistic quality of the delinquent subculture and is the clearest statement in the literature that a satisfactory theory of delinquency must make sense of these facts.

2. To justify the characterization of the delinquent subculture as "malicious" by multiplying citations from authorities would be empty pedantry. The malice is evident in any detailed description of juvenile gang life. We commend in particular, however, the cited works of Thrasher, Shaw and McKay and Robison *et al.* One aspect of this "gratuitous hostility" deserves spe-

cial mention, however, for the benefit of those who see in the provision of facilities for "wholesome recreation" some magical therapeutic virtue. "On entering a playground or a gym the first activity of gang members is to disrupt and interrupt whatever activities are going on. Nongang members flee, and when the coast is clear the gang plays desultorily on the apparatus or carries on horseplay." Sophia Robison *et al., op. cit.,* p. 159. See, to the same effect, the excellent little book by Kenneth H. Rogers, *Street Gangs in Toronto* (Toronto: The Ryerson Press, 1945), pp. 18-19.

3: Shaw and McKay, in their *Social Factors in Juvenile Delinquency,* p. 241, come very close to making this point quite explicitly: "In fact the standards of these groups may represent a complete reversal of the standards and norms of conventional society. Types of conduct which result in personal degradation and dishonor in a conventional group, serve to enhance and elevate the personal prestige and status of a member of the delinquent group."

4. *Federal Probation,* XVIII (March, 1954), 3-16 contains an extremely valuable symposium on vandalism, which highlights all of the characteristics we have imputed to the delinquent subculture. In the belief that no generalization can convey the flavor and scope of this subculture as well as a simple but massive enumeration, we quote at length from Joseph E. Murphy's contribution, pp. 8-9:

Studies of the complaints made by citizens and public officials reveal that hardly any property is safe from this form of aggression. Schools are often the object of attack by vandals. Windows are broken; records, books, desks, typewriters, supplies, and other equipment are stolen or destroyed. Public property of all types appears to offer peculiar allurement to children bent on destruction. Parks, playgrounds, highway signs, and markers are frequently defaced or destroyed. Trees, shrubs, flowers, benches, and other equipment suffer in like manner. Autoists are constantly reporting the slashing or releasing of air from tires, broken windows, stolen accessories. Golf clubs complain that benches, markers, flags, even expensive and difficult-to-replace putting greens are defaced, broken or uprooted. Libraries report the theft and destruction of books and other equipment. Railroads complain of and demand protection from the destruction of freight car seals, theft of property, willful and deliberate throwing of stones at passenger car windows, tampering with rails and switches. Vacant houses are always the particular delight of children seeking outlets for destructive instincts; windows are broken, plumbing and hardware stolen, destroyed, or rendered unusable. Gasoline operators report pumps and other service equipment stolen, broken, or destroyed. Theatre managers, frequently in the "better" neighborhoods, complain of the slashing of seats, willful damaging of toilet facilities, even the burning of rugs, carpets, etc.

Recently the Newark *Evening News,* commenting editorially on the problem of vandalism in New York City housing projects, stated "housing authorities complain of the tearing out of steel banisters, incinerator openings, and mail boxes, damaging of elevators, defacing walls, smashing windows and light bulbs, stealing nozzles of fire hoses, destroying trees and benches on the project's grounds and occasionally plundering and setting fire to parked cars. Moreover, gangs have terrorized not only tenants but also the three hundred unarmed watchmen hired to protect the property."

This quotation places "stealing" in the context of a host of other manifestations of the protean "orneriness" of which we have spoken. The implication is strong that the fact that an object is "stolen" rather than destroyed or damaged is, from the standpoint of motivation, almost incidental. J. P. Shalloo, *ibid.,* pp. 6-7, states in a forceful way the problem which this creates for criminological theory: "Delinquency and crime are, and have been regarded as, purposeful behavior. But wanton and vicious destruction of property both public and private by teen-age hoodlums reveals no purpose, no rhyme, no reason. . . . These are not the actions of thoughtless youth. These are actions based upon a calculated contempt for the rights of others . . ."

It is widely believed that vandalism, on the scale we know it today, is a relatively recent phenomenon. Douglas H. MacNeil, *ibid.,* p. 16, observes that, although vandalism is a form of delinquency which has been neglected by social scientists, there is little reason to believe that it has increased spectacularly, if at all, in recent years. Apparently it is and it has been for many years part and parcel, indeed the very spirit, of the delinquent subculture.

In connection with the versatility

of the delinquent subculture, it should be noted that truancy is also institutionalized in the delinquent gang. In Lester E. Hewitt and Richard L. Jenkins, *op. cit.,* p. 94, habitual truancy as found to have a tetrachoric coefficient of correlation of .10 with the "unsocialized aggressive" syndrome, -.08 with the "overinhibited behavior" syndrome and .75 with the "socialized delinquent" syndrome. These findings are of special interest because the latter syndrome corresponds closely to what we have called the delinquent subculture. For summaries of studies on the relationship between truancy and other forms of delinquency see Norman Fenton, *The Delinquent Boy and the Correctional School* (Claremont, California: Claremont Colleges Guidance Center, 1935), pp. 66-69 and William Kvaraceus, *Juvenile Delinquency and the School* (Yonkers-on-Hudson: World Book Company, 1945), pp. 144-146.

5. See the splendid report on "Working with a Street Gang" in Sylvan S. Furman (ed.), *Reaching the Unreached* (New York: New York City Youth Board, 1952), pp. 112-121. On this quality of short-run hedonism we quote, p. 13:

One boy once told me, "Now, for example, you take an average day. What happens? We come down to the restaurant and we sit in the restaurant, and sit and sit. All right, say, er . . . after a couple of hours in the restaurant, maybe we'll go to a poolroom, shoot a little pool, that's if somebody's got the money. O. K., a little pool, come back. By this time the restaurant is closed. We go in the candy store, sit around the candy store for a while, and that's it, that's all we do, man."

See also Barbara Bellow *et al.,* *op. cit.,* pp. 4-15, and Ruth Topping, *op. cit.,* p. 353.

6. The solidarity of the gang and the dependence of its members upon one another are especially well described in Barbara Bellow *et al., op. cit.,* p. 16 and Sophia Robison *et al., op. cit.,* p. 158.

7. See Clifford R. Shaw and Henry D. McKay, *Social Factors in Juvenile Delinquency,* p. 111.

8. See William Foote Whyte, "Social Organization in the Slums," *American Sociological Review,* VIII (February, 1943), 34-39.

9. See Clifford R. Shaw and Henry D. McKay, *op. cit.,* p. 115.

10. See Clifford R. Shaw and Henry D. McKay, *Juvenile Delinquency and Urban Areas,* pp. 180-181, Henry D. McKay, *op. cit.,* p. 35, and Robert K. Merton, "Social Structure and Anomie," *American Sociological Review,* III (October, 1938), 672-682.

11. On the sources of juvenile delinquency statistics and the problems of their interpretation see Sophia M. Robison, *Can Delinquency Be Measured?* (New York: Columbia University Press, 1936); Edward E. Schwarz, "Statistics of Juvenile Delinquency in the United States," *The Annals of the American Academy of Political and Social Science,* CCLXI (January, 1949), 9-20; Richard I. Perlman, "The Meaning of Juvenile Delinquency Statistics," *Federal Probation,* XIII (September, 1949), 63-67 and Paul W. Tappan, *Juvenile Delinquency,* (New York: McGraw-Hill Book Company, 1949), Chapters I and II.

CHAPTER III

1. Reference group theory, which is concerned with the determinants of our reference groups and with the ways in which our reference groups influence our action, is rapidly emerging as one of the most important areas of social psychological research. An excellent collection of papers on reference group theory may be found in Guy E. Swanson, Theodore M. Newcomb and Eugene L. Hartley (eds.), *Readings in Social Psychology* (New York: Henry Holt and Company, 1952), pp. 410-444. This volume contains many other excellent papers on the effects of group pressures upon the formation of norms and judgments. Of special importance are the papers by Muzafer Sherif, pp. 249-262 and S. E. Asch, pp. 2-11.

2. In the opinion of the writer there is no thoroughly satisfactory general treatment of the social psychology of crowd behavior, in the sense of a theoretical analysis which makes intelligible as well as describes the transformations of behavior which occur under crowd conditions. One of the better short treatments is Chapter 16 of Kimball Young, *Social Psychology* (New York: F. S. Crofts and Company, 1946). A thoughtful and stimulating discussion from the standpoint of modern learning theory will be found in Chapter 14 of Neal E.

Miller and John Dollard, *Social Learning and Imitation* (New Haven: Yale University Press, 1941). The most valuable extended analysis of mob behavior is Alfred M. Lee and Norman D. Humphrey, *Race Riot* (New York: Dryden Press, 1943).

In the literature on rumor we can also see at work many of the principles we have described here. We can see how rumors are collectively but unconsciously tailored to the needs and the problems of the public within which they spread, how common interests and established lines of communication determine the lines of diffusion, and how rumors are shaped and transformed in the communication process. The leading general treatise on rumor is Gordon W. Allport and Leo Postman, *The Psychology of Rumor* (New York: Henry Holt and Company, 1947). A most valuable and penetrating analysis of the history of a rumor is Leon Festinger, Dorwin Cartwright, Kathleen Bar-

ber *et al.*, "A Study of Rumor, Its Origin and Spread," *Human Relations*, I (August, 1948), 464-486.

3. An excellent treatise containing a number of detailed analyses of specific social movements is Hadley Cantril, *The Psychology of Social Movements* (New York: Wiley Book Company, 1941).

4. See Hadley Cantril, *op. cit.*, for several examples of such analyses. Liston Pope, *Millhands and Preachers* (New Haven: Yale University Press, 1942) is a remarkably acute sociological interpretation of the rise and differentiation of sects and denominations in our own society. On revivalistic and messianic movements in non-literate groups see Ralph Linton (ed.) *Acculturation in Seven American Indian Tribes* (New York: D. Appleton-Century Company, 1940), and Bernard Barber, "Acculturation and Messianic Movements," *American Sociological Review*, VI (October, 1941), 663-669.

CHAPTER IV

1. For a discussion of some of the ways in which life in the middle class generates its own characteristic problems of adjustment see Arnold Green, "The Middle Class Male Child and Neurosis," *American Sociological Review*, XI (February, 1946), 31-41. See also John Levy, "A Quantitative Study of the Relationship Between Intelligence and Economic Status As Factors in the Etiology of Children's Behavior Problems," *American Journal of Or-*

thopsychiatry, I (January, 1931), 152-162.

2. The literature on social class is very large and we shall list here only a few of the more useful references. An excellent general treatment of the meaning of social class and its relationship to kinship may be found in Talcott Parsons, "An Analytical Approach to the Theory of Social Stratification," *American Journal of Sociology*, XLV (May, 1940), 841-862. William Lloyd Warner has

been the most influential student of the social class systems of American communities. See W. Lloyd Warner and Associates, *Democracy in Jonesville* (New York: Harper and Brothers, 1949); W. Lloyd Warner and Paul S. Lunt, *The Social Life of a Modern Community* (New Haven: Yale University Press, 1941); and W. Lloyd Warner, Marcia Meeker and Kenneth Eells, *Social Class in America: A Manual of Procedure for the Measurement of Social Status* (Chicago: Science Research Associates, 1949). Wayne Wheeler's *Stratification in a Plains Community* (Minneapolis: 1949) is deserving of special mention because of its relatively exhaustive enumeration of the criteria of status in a brief space and its vivid description of those criteria in terms of the subjects' own colloquialisms. Other useful studies are Allison Davis, Burleigh B. Gardner and Mary R. Gardner, *Deep South: A Social Anthropological Study of Class and Caste* (Chicago: University of Chicago Press, 1941); James West, *Plainville, U. S. A.* (New York: Columbia University Press, 1945); and John Useem, Pierre Tangent and Ruth Useem, "Stratification in a Prairie Town," *American Sociological Review,* VII (June, 1942), 331-342.

3. On this "etiquette of deference in a democracy" see W. Lloyd Warner and Associates, *op. cit.,* p. 23, and James West, *op. cit.,* pp. 115-116.

4. R. H. Tawney, for example, in *Religion and the Rise of Capitalism* (New York: Penguin Books, 1947), pp. 27-28, writes of the Middle Ages:

The facts of class status and inequality were rationalized in the Middle Ages by a functional theory of society ... Each member has its own function, prayer, or defense, or merchandise or tilling the soil. Each must receive the means suited to its station, and must claim no more. Within classes there must be equality; if one takes into his hand the living of the two, his neighbor will go short. Between classes there must be inequality; for otherwise it cannot perform its function, or— a strange thought to us—enjoy its rights. Peasants must not encroach on those above them. Lords must not despoil peasants. Craftsmen and merchants must receive what will maintain them in their calling, and no more.

And Ruth Benedict, in *The Chrysanthemum and the Sword* (Boston: Houghton Mifflin Company, 1946), pp. 148-150, writes of Japan:

Giri [duty] to one's name also requires that one live according to one's station in life. If a man fails in this giri he has no right to respect himself. This means in Tokugawa times that he accepted as part of his self-respect the detailed sumptuary laws which regulated practically everything he wore or had or used. Americans are shocked to the core by laws which define these things by inherited class rights. Self-respect in America is bound up with improving one's status and fixed sumptuary laws are a denial of the very basis of our society ... In Japan getting rich is under suspicion and maintaining proper station is not. Even today the poor as well as the rich invest their self-respect in observing the conventions of hierarchy. It is a virtue alien to America.

5. See Max Weber, *The Protestant Ethic and the Spirit of Capitalism,* tr. by Talcott Parsons (London: George Allen and Unwin, 1930).

6. We will attempt no point by point documentation of this description. It is based on induction from a voluminous literature on social class and socialization in America, and almost every source we refer to in this chapter is relevant to this description. Two items which merit special mention, however, are Kingsley Davis, "Mental Hygiene and the Class Structure," *Psychiatry,* I (February, 1938), 55-65 and Margaret Mead, *And Keep Your Powder Dry* (New York: William Morrow and Company, 1942).

7. The principal sources of our description of the working class as a "cultural setting" are the cited works of E. Wight Bakke and Allison Davis. On social class differences in child-rearing practices, there are, in addition to incidental and scattered materials in general works on social class, the following studies which are more specifically and systematically concerned with these class differences: The pioneer work is John E. Anderson, *The Young Child in the Home,* a report of the Committee on the Infant and Preschool Child of the White House Conference on Child Health and Protection (New York: D. Appleton-Century, 1936). Other statistical studies are Allison Davis and Robert J. Havighurst, "Social-Class and Color Differences in Child-Rearing," *American Sociological Review,* XI (December, 1946), 698-710 and Martha C. Ericson, "Child-Rearing and Social Status," *American Journal of Sociology,* LIII (November, 1946), 190-192. Other

major contributions are Allison Davis and John Dollard, *Children of Bondage* (Washington, D. C.: American Council on Education, 1940); Allison Davis, Burleigh Gardner and Mary R. Gardner, *op. cit.,* especially pp. 102-106 and 129-133; Allison Davis, "Socialization and Adolescent Personality," in Guy E. Swanson, Theodore M. Newcomb and Eugene L. Hartley (eds.), *Readings in Social Physchology* (New York: Henry Holt and Company, 1952), pp. 520-531. For a highly readable, non-technical summary of most of the foregoing literature see Allison Davis and Robert J. Havighurst, *Father of the Man* (Boston: Houghton Mifflin Company, 1947).

8. These expressions, the "ethic of individual responsibility" and the "ethic of reciprocity," are our own. The ideas they signify, however, are derived from the cited paper of Allison Davis, "The Motivation of the Underprivileged Worker," and William F. Whyte, *Street Corner Society* (Chicago: University of Chicago Press, 1937).

9. See the special issue of *The Journal of Social Issues,* V (Winter, 1949) on "Participation, Culture and Personality," especially the articles by Morris Rosenberg, pp. 14-23, Seymour Bellin and Frank Riessman, Jr., pp. 24-32 and Bruce F. Young and Morris Rosenberg, pp. 42-45.

10. *Woman's Day* is a magazine distributed through the A & P food stores and addressed to the problems and interests of housewives. Its articles on child care are clearly written from a "correct" middle-class perspective. The following paragraphs on a child's "typical day"

are quoted here not as a contribution to the scientific literature on socialization but as a datum illustrative of middle-class expectations regarding children. They are intended to impress the reader of *Woman's Day* with the number of demands which are placed on our children and to suggest that we "temper our expectations to their age and abilities." The point of particular interest to us, however, is that the article seems to take for granted the inevitability of most of these demands; it shows no awareness that, for the vast majority of *working-class* children, this "typical day" is most *untypical*. The excerpt is from Bess B. Lane, "Is Childhood Carefree?", *Woman's Day*, February, 1949) 40.

The after-school hours are likely to be almost as crowded [as the school hours]. There are school clubs. There are special lessons such as music and dancing. There are assignments for homework. There are also home duties to be performed, such as table setting and dish washing. All these activities, combined with occasional trips to the doctor, the dentist, the department store, the library, the museum, the movies, pretty well fill the hours between school and bedtime. Almost no time is left for the nothing-at-all which most children need and enjoy.

In addition to the large number of demands on the child's time and energy, there are innumerable expectations, spoken and implied, which bear heavily upon him. The adult can do well in one field of knowledge and get by, but the child is expected to get along with many different ages and many different personalities, in the home, the school and elsewhere. And toward all these people he must be generous and thoughtful or he is not a "good" boy.

11. See Harrison G. Gough, "The Relationship of Socio-Economic Status to Personality Inventory and Achievement Scores," *Journal of Educational Psychology*, XXXVII (December, 1946), 527-540 and a series of studies by Robert J. Havighurst and Associates, "Relations between Ability and Social Status in a Midwestern Community," *Journal of Educational Psychology*, XXXV (May, 1944), 357-368; XXXVI (October, 1945), 499-509, XXXVIII (April, 1947), 241-247 and XXXVIII (November, 1947), 437-442. A convenient and authoritative summary of the findings in this area is a little book by Allison Davis, *Social-Class Influences upon Learning* (Cambridge: Harvard University Press, 1948).

12. Most of the books on social class and on socialization contain incidental and scattered observations on class-typical personalities and the socialization literature seems to take for granted that the socialization disciplines characteristic of the different social classes actually produce significantly different personality types. The books cited in this section are among the few, however, which are specifically and directly concerned with personality differences and which present concrete research data bearing upon the subject rather than just diffuse impressions.

13. The research was designed and carried out by Miss Barker under the supervision of the present writer. The subjects consisted of all the white boys, aged 13-16, in a junior high school in an Indiana city

of 40,000 population. The determination of social class was based primarily on father's occupation. In general, the middle-class parents were professionals, proprietors and managers of well-known business firms and highly skilled clerical and kindred workers. The working-class parents were largely unskilled and semi-skilled workers in local factories and service workers in a local college and mental institution.

14. See, for example, the following statements by educators: Elizabeth M. Fuller, Helen Christianson, Neith Headley *et al.*, "Practices and Resources in Early Childhood Education," in *The Forty-Sixth Yearbook of the National Society for the Study of Education*, Part II (Chicago: University of Chicago Press, 1947), pp. 103-105 and Samuel Smith, George R. Cressman and Robert K. Speer, *Education and Society: An Introduction to Education for a Democracy* (New York: The Dryden Press, 1942), pp. 154-155.

15. On the mental hygiene implications of failure in conforming to teacher expectations, see Fritz Redl and William W. Wattenberg, *Mental Hygiene in Teaching* (New York: D. Appleton-Century Company, 1940), pp. 245-247; and an excellent short article by Roger G. Barker, "Success and Failure in the Classroom," in Wayne Dennis (ed.), *Readings in Child Psychology* (New York: Prentice-Hall, Inc., 1951), pp. 577-582, reprinted from an article in *Progressive Education*, XIX (1942), 221-224.

16. W. Lloyd Warner, Robert J. Havighurst and Martin B. Loeb, *Who Shall Be Educated?* (New York: Harper and Brothers, 1944), is an excellent discussion of the way

in which school policy is shaped by middle-class values. The functions of teachers, they say, are two: "They train or seek to train children in middle-class manners and skills. And they select those children from the middle and lower classes who appear to be the best candidates for promotion in the social hierarchy." (p. 107). A public-school superintendent, critical of current guidance philosophy, states: "Boards of Education and Parent-Teacher Associations are invariably Calvinists. . . . They believe that a Director of Guidance in the high school will be able to elevate every student, that is, to lead him into some pleasant and dignified occupation, to guide him so that his will not be a life of toil or manual work or degrading forms of labor. A school with a real guidance program should raise all pupils to a high social and economic position." Ernest W. Butterfield, "Our White-Collar Guidance Psychology," *The Clearing House*, XIII (May, 1939), 516.

17. Percival M. Symonds, "Personality Adjustment of Women Teachers," *American Journal of Orthopsychiatry*, XI (January, 1941), 15, comments, on the basis of a study of 50 biographies of women teachers:

> It is because the need for achievement is so strong among teachers that competition is used as a motivating force so widely in schools. The teacher with strong drive for achievement is likely to overstimulate the bright, and show unjust discrimination against the dull and failing.

18. The best study is E. Koster Wickman, *Children's Behavior and*

Teachers' Attitudes (New York: The Commonwealth Fund, 1928). The findings of later studies are consistent with Wickman's. See Harold H. Anderson, "The Construction of a Mental Hygiene Scale for Teachers," *American Journal of Orthopsychiatry*, X (April, 1940), 253-263, and Grace B. Cox and Harold H. Anderson, "A Study of Teachers' Responses to Problem Situations As Reported by Teachers and Students," *American Journal of Orthopsychiatry*, XIV (July, 1944), 528-544.

19. See William F. Whyte, *op. cit., passim,* but especially pp. 98-104. See also E. L. Johnstone, "What Do Boys Think of Us—and Why?", *Proceedings of the American Prison Association, 1944* (New York: The American Prison Association, 1944), pp. 143-144.

20. There is tangible research evidence that, at least in the school area, low status is accompanied by maladjustment. Joel B. Montague, "Social Status and Adjustment in School," *Clearing House,* XXVII (September, 1952), 19-24, investigates the relationship between the adjustment of students and the students' own estimates of the status of their parents in the community. The lowest status group, in contrast to the middle and upper status groups, strikingly more often, in response to an attitude questionnaire, indicate that school is not interesting, the studies are too hard, they don't like their courses, they are not popular, they are left out of things, it is hard to make friends, they are unable to express themselves well, they can't seem to concentrate, there is not enough time to study. Onas Scandrette, "School—through the Eyes of the Underchosen," in the same issue of *Clearing House,* 35-37, compares the attitudes of children who are frequently chosen and those who are underchosen by their classmates to be members of a classroom project committee. The underchosen are much more likely to feel that teachers have little personal interest in their students, teachers are unfair, teachers are unkind, teachers are unfriendly, other students are unkind, association with the opposite sex is not enjoyable, school work is too hard.

CHAPTER V

1. No single strand of our argument concerning the motivation of the delinquent subculture is entirely original. All have been at least adumbrated and some quite trenchantly formulated by others.

The idea that aggressive behavior, including crime and delinquency, are often reactions to difficulties in achieving status in legitimate status systems has been remarked by many, although the systematic linkage between the particular status problems we have described and social class position has not been well developed in the literature. Caroline B. Zachry, for example, in *Emotion and Conduct in Adolescence* (New York: D. Appleton-Century Company, 1940), pp. 187, 200-209, 245-246, has a thoughtful discussion of the ego-damage resulting from inability to compete effectively in school and of the function of aggressive behavior in maintaining self-esteem. Arthur L. Wood, in "Social Disorganization and Crime," *Encyclopedia of Criminology* (New York: Philosophical Library, 1949), pp. 466-471, states that the highest crime rates tend to occur in those minority culture groups "which have become acculturated to the majority-group patterns of behavior, but due to hostility toward them they have failed to succeed in compation for social status." Robert B. Zajonc, in "Aggressive Attitudes of the 'Stranger' as a Function of Conformity Pressures," *Human Relations*, V (1952), 205-216, has experimentally tested the general hypothesis, although not in connection with delinquency or crime, that a "need to conform" with a pattern of behavior coupled with inability to conform successfully generates hostile attitudes towards that pattern.

The general notion of negativism as an ego-salving type of reaction-formation, which plays such an important part in the theory we have outlined, is common in the psychoanalytical literature. It has been brilliantly developed with specific reference to criminality in a paper by George Devereux, "Social Negativism and Criminal Psychopathology," *Journal of Criminal Psychopathology*, I (April, 1940), 322-338 and applied to other behavior problems in George Devereux and Malcolm E. Moos, "The Social Structure of Prisons, and the Organic Tensions," *Journal of Criminal Psychopathology*, IV (October, 1942), 306-324.

2. The distinguished criminologist, Sutherland, apparently had this in mind when he wrote: "It is not necessary that there be bad boys inducing good boys to commit offenses. It is generally a mutual stimulation, as a result of which each of the boys commits delinquencies which he would not commit alone." Edwin H. Sutherland, *Principles of Criminology* (New York: J. B. Lippincott Company, 1947), p. 145. Having made the point, however, Sutherland failed to develop its implications, and in his general theory of criminal behavior the function of the group or the gang is not collectively to *contrive* delinquency but merely to *transmit* the delinquent tradition and to provide protection to the members of the group. Fritz Redl, on the other hand, in "The Psychology of Gang Formation and the Treatment of Juvenile Delinquents," *The Psychoanalytic Study of the Child, Vol I,* (New York: International Universities Press, 1945), pp. 367-377, has developed at considerable length the ways in which the group makes possible for its members behavior which would otherwise not be available to them.

3. Our argument to this point owes much to George H. Grosser, *Juvenile Delinquency and Contemporary American Sex Roles* (Unpublished Ph. D. Dissertation, Harvard University, 1952). This dissertation is the most thorough discussion in the literature of sex differences in delinquency.

4. John Levy classified into "personality and emotional problems" and "delinquency" (or "social problems") the conduct disorders of 700 children referred to the Institute for Juvenile Research in Chicago. He found that "socially high grade children have personality or emotional problems, whereas the chil-

dren belonging to the lower classes have social problems." He argues that economic status is not so important in determining the type of "problem" a child becomes as is intelligence, which is correlated with both economic status and type of problem. In any event, it is clear that the probabilities of developing particular types of conduct disorders depend upon some—and probably several—class-linked variables. See John Levy, "A Quantitative Study of the Relationship between Intelligence and Economic Status as Factors in the Etiology of Children's Behavior Problems," *American Journal of Orthopsychiatry,* I (January, 1931), 152-162.

5. See, for example, the psychoanalytical classic, Franz Alexander and William Healy, *Roots of Crime,* (New York: Alfred A. Knopf, 1935), pp. 282 ff. These authors were struck by certain characteristic differences between American and European criminals who had been psychoanalytically studied. They were especially impressed by the tendency in America "to display one's masculinity by showing disrespect for law." This motive was not nearly so prominent in the European cases. Since Alexander himself participated in both the European and American studies, it is probable that the differences are not the result of the theoretical biases of the investigators but reflect real differences in the populations from which the cases were drawn.

6. Some of these differences be-

tween children of the different social classes are discussed in Meyer Raban, "Sex-Role Identification in Young Children in Two Diverse Social Groups," *Genetic Psychological Monographs,* XLII (1950), 81-158. This monograph also contains references to other literature on the subject.

7. However, the author has been informed that a study is now under way in Chicago, under the auspices of the Institute for Juvenile Research, with the object of determining the nature and the extent of the delinquencies of *all* the children in a selected neighborhood. Although the official records of all the boys will be available to the investigators, the differentiation of the population into categories of delinquents and non-delinquents will be based primarily on independent investigation by field workers dealing directly with the boys concerned.

8. The most massive and expensive study of delinquency by the paired comparison method is that of Sheldon and Eleanor Glueck, *Unraveling Juvenile Delinquency* (New York: Commonwealth Fund, 1950). Five hundred institutionalized delinquents were compared with five hundred non-delinquents and conclusions drawn about the characteristics of delinquents and the determinants of delinquency. See the criticisms of this study by Sol Rubin and by Albert J. Reiss, Jr. in *The American Journal of Sociology,* LVII (September, 1951), 107-120.

Index